TWO GREAT REBEL ARMIES

Two Great Rebel Armies

AN ESSAY IN CONFEDERATE MILITARY HISTORY

RICHARD M. McMURRY

The University of North Carolina Press
Chapel Hill & London

Printed in the United States of America

Library of Congress Cataloging-in-Publication Data

McMurry, Richard M.
Two great rebel armies: an essay in Confederate
military history / Richard M. McMurry.
p.   cm.
Bibliography: p.
Includes index.
ISBN-13: 978-0-8078-1819-0 (cloth: alk. paper)
ISBN-13: 978-0-8078-4569-1 (pbk.: alk. paper)
1. Confederate States of America. Army—History. 2. Confederate
States of America. Army of Northern Virginia—History.
3. Confederate States of America. Army of Tennessee—History.
4. United States—History—Civil War, 1861–1865—Campaigns.
I. Title.
E545.M37 1989   88-14374
973.7'42—dc19   CIP

FOR BELL WILEY,

teacher and friend

Contents

Preface

everal years ago, after completing a biography of Confederate General John Bell Hood, I began work on a history of the Atlanta Campaign of 1864—a then much-neglected military operation that had been very important in the American Civil War. After several months' work on the project, I found myself completely bogged down in what was rapidly becoming a three-hundred-page introduction to chapter one of a history of the Atlanta Campaign.

When two other starts produced similar results, I realized that it was going to be impossible to complete the study I envisioned without going into so much background material that the introductory section would constitute a separate book. Such a study would inevitably embrace far more than a simple narrative of the 1864 struggle for Atlanta. It would have to include a detailed examination of the Federal and Confederate armies in the winter of 1863–64 and of their preparations for the campaign of the following spring and summer. Such a discussion would cover in detail their organizations, their leaders, their personnel, and the overall political and strategic situation in which they found themselves in the spring and summer of 1864.

More work along these lines led to similar problems. It was simply impossible to discuss intelligently the situation in the winter of 1863–64 without going back to the events that took place in the fall of 1863. Coverage of those events, in turn, necessitated a discussion of what had happened in the preceding summer. Eventually, by following this process, I reached the spring of 1862 and was, I thought, ready to begin to write my history of the Atlanta Campaign. Again, however, it soon became obvious that I needed to go back even earlier. Many of the factors—both bad and good—that hampered or helped the two armies struggling in North Georgia in 1864 had their origins in the months before the spring of 1862 when those armies clashed in their first great battle at Shiloh. Many of the factors went back to the first days of the war, and some of them could be traced far back into the antebellum years.

This realization led to the development of a new plan that would both curtail and expand the study. I decided to limit the coverage to the Confederate side but to widen the scope of the work so as to embrace the political, economic, strategic, tactical, organizational, administrative, naval, and logistical facets of the Confederacy's war on the western front from the time of secession in 1861 to the end of the war in 1865. Although the focus of the study would be on the Confederates' main western military force—the Army of Tennessee—the sweep of the work would be broad enough to cover in some detail the area from the Appalachian Mountains on the east to the Ozarks on the west and from the Ohio and Missouri rivers on the north to the Gulf of Mexico on the south. The work would bear the title "Steps Marked in Blood: The Confederacy's War in the West."

It did not matter that the research and writing would constantly be interrupted by other projects (as, indeed, they have been) or that a work on so vast a subject would probably never be completed. Historical research, as my friend Arnold Shankman once remarked, is supposed to be fun. To those of us who have been converted to its study, the western front of the American Civil War was, by far, the most important part of that struggle. Knowledge of its history is of primary importance in our efforts to understand the course of the conflict. The study of its history is time-consuming, frustrating, expensive, and exhausting—but it is also fun.

One writer on the Rebels' western army has said that his idea of heaven is to be able to sit around and talk with the generals who were in the Army of Tennessee and to find out from them what actually had happened at Shiloh, Perryville, Cassville, Spring Hill, and several other points on that ill-starred army's odyssey across the western Confederacy. Such a hope, of course, is predicated upon the shaky assumption that at least some of the generals who served with the Army of Tennessee are in heaven. Since Larry Daniel, the historian who made the statement, is also a theologian, I prefer not to debate the point with him.

ANYONE who deals in more than a cursory way with the military aspect of the Southern side of the Civil War must, sooner or later, come to grips with Robert E. Lee, his role in the war, and his dominant place in Confederate historiography. During the war, Lee became the hope of the Confederacy, and in the years since the conflict closed he, far more than any other man, came to symbolize what white Southerners liked to believe the Confederacy had been.

In the decades after the war, interest in Confederate military history tended to focus on Lee and his Army of Northern Virginia and their campaigns and battles. The Southern forces that had fought outside the Old Dominion were, for the most part, neglected. Northern as well as Southern writers have usually devoted most of their time and energy to studying the war in Virginia. The towering presence of Lee and the veneration in which he has been held by both Northerners and Southerners in large part account for the skewing of Rebel military history toward the fighting in the East. Even John Fiske, a self-confessed "Connecticut Yankee" and one of the few early writers to appreciate the importance of the war in the West, admitted in 1900 that he reverently removed his hat when he passed the statue of Lee in New Orleans—a gesture that reminds one of Douglas Southall Freeman's practice of saluting whenever he drove past the great equestrian statue of Lee that stands on Monument Avenue in Richmond.

In addition to wrestling with the Lee problem, those of us who study the war in the West must also decide what we think about the provocative and controversial ideas put forth over the last two decades by Thomas Lawrence Connelly. Since many of Connelly's more polemical and disputed ideas concern Lee, his role in

Confederate military history, and his standing in both Southern and national historical literature, these two problems are not unrelated.

As explained in Chapter 9, this book had its beginnings in an effort to focus my ideas about several of the points raised by Connelly in his various assaults on Lee and his reputation. In one sense, then, this book is, in part, an effort to straighten out my own thinking on the subject and to clear the decks of the debris and clutter left by Connelly's foray against Lee. In so doing, I hope to remove some of the impediments to the writing of "Steps Marked in Blood."

A third major problem with which anyone studying the western Confederates must deal is the necessity of explaining their almost unbroken string of defeats. John Fiske pointed out in the late nineteenth century in a series of lectures and later in *The Mississippi Valley in the Civil War* that myopically focusing on the war in Virginia produces a very distorted picture of Confederate military history. One would conclude from a study of events in Virginia from 1861 to 1864 that the South's military effort was faring well in the first three years of the war and that the Rebels were holding their own, hurling back one invading Yankee army after another. If one proceeds on that assumption, the sudden collapse of the Confederate position in the spring of 1865 comes as something of a shock.

Fiske believed—correctly—that a true picture of the war could emerge only from a study of the western operations. In that vast theater the Confederate cause went steadily downhill from the day of its birth in the spring of 1861. The long, bloody campaigns that ended with the surrender of the Army of Tennessee at Bennett's Farm, near Durham Station, North Carolina, in April 1865, began in Missouri, Arkansas, Kentucky, and Tennessee four years earlier. The collapse of the Confederacy was no sudden, surprising phenomenon; it was a slow but steady process. It seems, in fact, that by the spring of 1861 the Army of Tennessee—which had not then even formally come into existence—had already passed the point of no return on the road to Bennett's Farm. The Army of Northern Virginia was an aberration in Confederate military history because of its success.

In part, then, this book is also my attempt to develop and draw together some ideas about the reasons for the Rebels' almost complete lack of success in the West and to contrast their experiences there with the relative success they enjoyed on the eastern front in Virginia. By so doing, I hope to outline a large part of the scaffolding that will be used during the writing of various parts of "Steps Marked in Blood." In effect, then, this book is a philosophical and historiographical introduction to the larger work that is yet to come.

IT seemed that the best way to achieve my goals was to compare the Army of Tennessee and the Army of Northern Virginia. My hope was to develop a discussion of those factors in Confederate military history that applied to one of the two great Rebel armies but not to the other or that affected them in different ways or to different degrees. Thus, for example, the theory advanced by Grady McWhiney and Perry D. Jamieson in *Attack and Die: Civil War Military Tactics and the Southern Heritage* (University, Ala., 1982) that Confederate defeat was the result of the Southerners' proclivity for outmoded offensive tactics and that that proclivity was the product of the Rebels' Celtic ancestry is irrelevant to this essay. The theory that Celtic corpuscles coursing through Rebel veins led to the defeat of the Confederacy—whatever its validity—is equally applicable to the Army of Tennessee and the Army of Northern Virginia.

A somewhat different problem arose with *Why the South Lost the Civil War* by Richard E. Beringer, Herman Hattaway, Archer Jones, and William N. Still, Jr. (Athens, Ga., 1986). The authors of *Why the South Lost* argue that the Rebels' fatal weakness was their poorly developed sense of Confederate nationalism. Their nationalism was strong enough to create the Confederacy and to sustain it through the first three years of the war but too weak to stand up in the face of the military defeats the Southerners suffered beginning in 1864. In effect, the authors of *Why the South Lost* argue the irrefutable thesis that the Rebels lost the war because their armies lost the battles. A weak sense of nationalism was a burden for both the Army of Tennessee and the Army of Northern Virginia and therefore not germane to this book. In truth, however, only one of the two major Southern armies lost the battles (a fact with which Beringer, Hattaway, Jones, and Still do not deal). It began losing them in 1861, and it continued to do so up until the end of the war. I, therefore, am dealing with a different problem than that addressed by the authors of *Why the South Lost*.

The plan to form this book around a comparison of the two most important Rebel armies, however, quickly led to a problem. Although I set out to compare the two Southern armies, I often wound up comparing "the West" or "the western Confederates"—and not the Army of Tennessee per se—with the Army of Northern Virginia, or "the East," or "the eastern Confederates."

As it turned out, this was not a serious difficulty. The problem was more methodological than real, and for three reasons I made no serious attempt to avoid it. First, the fate of the Army of Tennessee was always inextricably linked with the larger fate of the western Confederacy. Second, on three occasions, the Rebel government created more or less formal administrative structures that united the Army of Tennessee in one way or another with most of the other Confederate forces operating in the West and sometimes in the Trans-Mississippi as well. Finally, the Army of Tennessee eventually absorbed almost all of the other Confederate troops in the West. For these reasons, I decided not to waste time trying to draw a mostly artificial distinction between the Army of Tennessee and the West but to treat them separately when such an approach was possible and desirable and to deal with them jointly when the subject under discussion warranted such treatment or when it was impossible to separate them.

SEVERAL friends have been associated in one way or another with this project. Tom Connelly, to whom all students of the western Confederacy owe a great debt, originated and expounded many of the ideas that served as the catalysts (and targets) for this book. He also heard a paper that I delivered at the 1986 Midwest Civil War Conference in Cincinnati and proposed that the paper be expanded into a book. Without Tom's suggestion, it is doubtful that *Two Great Rebel Armies* would ever have been anything more than an article in some obscure historical journal. Albert Castel, of Western Michigan University, in his spirited response to Connelly's theories, stressed ideas that helped to shape much of my thinking. Both Tom Connelly and Albert Castel are friends of mine, and I hope that I have been fair to them in these pages.

Several other friends have generously contributed their time and knowledge to improve this book. Larry Daniel, who, like the Bishop General Leonidas Polk, occasionally leaves his flock to stalk across the western battlefields, was kind enough to read an earlier draft and to make several useful suggestions. (In Larry's case, the flock is at St. Marks United Methodist Church in Memphis.)

Bob Krick, well-known raconteur of the Army of Northern Virginia and a self-described "compulsive nit-picker," went through the manuscript with a thoroughness equaled only by that with which he goes over the eastern battlefields whenever he ventures out of his lair at the Fredericksburg-Spotsylvania National Military Park. He detected many upside-down periods and other egregious blunders and made several valuable recommendations for improving the manuscript.

Dick Sommers, of the Army Military History Institute at Carlisle Barracks, Pennsylvania, struggled through an earlier version of the manuscript and flew to his typewriter to peck out a long letter full of helpful suggestions. He also went carefully through the text and littered its pages with even more comments than did Colonel Krick.

Gary Gallagher, of Pennsylvania State University, somehow managed to ignore Joe Paterno's mighty football team long enough to read the manuscript and to offer several pages of welcome suggestions. In his capacity as consultant for Civil War books at the University of North Carolina Press, Gary was also instrumental in bringing about the publication of the work.

What Larry Daniel, Bob Krick, Dick Sommers, and Gary Gallagher do not know about the Civil War is not worth knowing. To each of them I owe a great debt. As they would be the first to point out, however, they are not responsible for errors of fact or interpretation that remain. Sometimes—and it was always with fear and trepidation—I chose not to follow their suggestions.

Two Great Rebel Armies

CHAPTER ONE

Two Great Armies

During the American Civil War the Confederate government organized at least twenty-five field armies. Most of these forces—such as the Army of New River and the Army of East Florida—were small commands that were in existence for only short periods of time. Two of the Rebel armies, however, were in being for virtually the entire war and were indispensable to the Southern war effort. "You must remember," a Northern officer wrote in March 1865, "the Confederacy, its government, its territory, its every thing is concentrated in these two armies."[1]

One of these essential forces was the Army of Tennessee, which was known during its early months as the Army of the Mississippi. It was formally organized at Corinth, Mississippi, in the late winter and spring of 1862, when scattered military units were pulled together from all over the Old Southwest to try to recoup the Confederacy's recent losses in Kentucky and Tennessee. This army was first used to defend the area between the Appalachian Mountains and the Mississippi River, but by the late summer of 1862 it was committed to protecting the Nashville-Chattanooga-Atlanta backbone of the Confederacy. It acquired its second and more famous name in a November 1862 reorganization, when the new name was deemed more appropriate to its new mission.

During the war the Army of Tennessee campaigned over a vast area. Counting those from its predecessor units, its wartime dead are buried in Missouri, Arkansas, Kentucky, Louisiana, and every Confederate state east of the Mississippi. It was the mainstay of the Confederacy in the great theater of operations between the Appalachian Mountains and the Mississippi River that was known during the 1860s as the West.

The other important Rebel force was the Army of Northern Virginia—originally called the Army of the Potomac. This army was formed in the first spring and summer of the war near Manassas Junction, Virginia—born, wrote Douglas Southall Freeman, its greatest historian, "July 20, 1861, on the Plains of Manassas." It acquired its more famous name in the spring of 1862, and it spent the war campaigning in Virginia, Maryland, and Pennsylvania. The Army of Northern Virginia was the Confederacy's main strength in the area east of the Appalachians.[2]

The wartime experiences of these two great Rebel armies were quite different, and those differences have carried over into their treatment by historians. The Army of Northern Virginia won a series of breathtaking victories in 1861, 1862, and 1863, and it fought gallantly against great odds in 1864 and 1865 before being compelled to surrender to "overwhelming numbers and resources" on 9 April 1865. Its battles and leaders have become fixtures of United States history, and it would be difficult to find an educated American who has never heard of Robert E. Lee, Thomas J. "Stonewall" Jackson, Pickett's charge, and Appomattox. Two of its generals—Lee and Jackson—have been commemorated on United States postage stamps, an honor not bestowed upon any other officers who led armies against the country. When the great memorial carving was put on the side of Stone Mountain in Georgia, the same two generals, along with Rebel President Jefferson Davis, were chosen to represent the Confederacy (eventually the carving itself was depicted on both another United States postage stamp and a commemorative coin).

Virginia, wrote William Swinton, an early historian of the conflict, was "the main seat of war," where "the chief armies of the North and the South fought the war of secession to an issue." The Army of Northern Virginia he called "the chief armed force of secession." It was "that body of incomparable infantry," which

Two Great Armies

"for four years carried the . . . [Confederacy] on its bayonets." The Rebels' eastern army will forever be identified with—if not as—the Confederacy's effort to establish its independence.[3]

The Army of Tennessee, on the other hand, was sometimes ignored by the Confederate government during the war. It won only one major victory, and for that triumph—at Chickamauga, in Georgia, in September 1863—it had the not inconsiderable help of two divisions from the Army of Northern Virginia. During the war, the Army of Tennessee often faded from the popular mind, and today only dedicated students of the conflict are familiar with Leonidas Polk, Braxton Bragg, Resaca, and Bennett's Farm. For many years the Army of Tennessee was all but ignored, even by historians of the war. So bad was the situation that in 1941 Stanley F. Horn, author of the first book-length history of the Rebels' chief western force, protested in the Foreword to his work: "But all of the War Between the States was not fought in Virginia. There was another Confederate army, strangely neglected by most historians of the war—the Army of Tennessee. It too carried the fortunes of the Confederacy on its bayonets no less valiantly than its more famous sister army in Virginia."[4]

A random survey of a few recently published American history textbooks indicated that Horn's plea has fallen on deaf ears. The survey revealed that about 60 percent of the space devoted to Civil War land military operations was given over to the eastern theater of the war and about 40 percent was taken up with coverage of the West. (The Trans-Mississippi, the other area of major land operations, was totally ignored.) The survey also revealed that most of the space devoted to the eastern campaigns dealt with the Confederates, but most of the attention given to the West was focused on the Federals. This last fact may indicate that when textbook writers do deal with Civil War military operations they prefer to emphasize those armies that were more successful.

The authors of the textbooks at least mentioned all of the Rebels who commanded the major Southern forces, but their treatment of the two armies was uneven. Five subordinate Confederate generals of the eastern army were mentioned—Barnard E. Bee, Stonewall Jackson, James E. B. ("Jeb") Stuart, George E. Pickett, and James Longstreet.[5] By contrast, only two western subordinate generals, Nathan Bedford Forrest and Joseph Wheeler, were deemed important enough to be named in the textbooks. There was also a tendency to treat one or two of the eastern battles—notably First Manassas and Gettysburg—in some detail. In one case the surrender of the Army of Northern Virginia was covered in the text, but if unknowing readers did not spot a brief notation on a map, they might well believe that the war in the West was still going on.

This East-West disparity also permeates some more specialized works. Thomas H. O'Connor devoted three chapters of *The Disunited States: The Era of Civil War and Reconstruction* to an account of the war years. Almost two-thirds (65.2 percent) of the space devoted to a narrative of military events is given over to an account of the eastern battles. Gettysburg is covered in four pages; Vicksburg in one and a half. O'Connor even mislabels the Rebels' major western force, calling it "the Army of the Tennessee"—a title that, in fact, was borne by one of the Yankee armies in the West.[6]

The emphasis on the struggle in Virginia has been so pervasive that Appomattox has become synonymous with the end of the war. In its 1968 report to Congress the United States Civil War Centennial Commission published a photograph of Ulysses S. Grant III and Robert E. Lee IV shaking hands at the reconstructed McLean House at Appomattox, Virginia, where, according to the caption, "their forebears a century earlier ended the Civil War."

Quick perusal of the 1978 *Random House Dictionary* revealed only five entries relating to the Confederacy: "Appomattox," "Confederate States of America," "Davis, Jefferson," "Gettysburg," and "Lee, Robert E." The "Appomattox" entry reads as follows: "a town in central Virginia where Lee surrendered to [Lieutenant General Ulysses S.] Grant, ending the Civil War." Never mind that the Army of Tennessee fought on for more than two weeks after the Army of Northern Virginia had surrendered at Appomattox and that other Rebel forces continued the struggle longer still.[7]

In *Army of the Heartland: The Army of Tennessee, 1861–1862*, Thomas Lawrence Connelly cataloged five reasons why the western Rebel army has suffered both popular and scholarly neglect. One is what Connelly calls the "Lee tradition" in Southern historical writing. Some of the best and best-written books about the Confederate side of the war have come from the pens of such historians as Douglas Southall Freeman and Clifford Dowdey—men who were themselves Virginia gentlemen of the old school, whose version of the Confederacy pretty much followed the boundaries of the Old Dominion and who deified General Robert E. Lee and some of the other officers who served with the Army of Northern Virginia. Freeman, for example, once wrote an essay entitled "Southern Resources of Command" in which he discussed the Virginians who, as of early 1861, had had military experience and who might reasonably have been counted upon to offer their services to the state (or, as Freeman would have put it, "the State"). Although Freeman did mention a few officers from other states, he did so only to speculate about their availability for service in the Old Dominion. Even James H. Brewer's *The Confederate Negro* carries the subtitle *Virginia's Craftsmen and Military Laborers, 1861–1865*. Like many people, both Freeman and Brewer see Southern and Confederate history as the story of the Old Dominion expanded across Dixie.[8]

The Lee tradition early became united with the long-standing plantation myth to create the image of the Army of Northern Virginia as a group of cavaliers whose gallantry, chivalry, education, heritage, wealth, background, knightly manners, courage, and "breeding" set them apart from and a notch or two above other Americans and even other Southerners. Lee's men in Virginia were romanticized and made the epitome of what white Southerners fancied themselves to be. This vision was not limited to Southerners or even to Americans. G. F. R. Henderson, an Englishman and an early biographer of Stonewall Jackson, wrote of Lee's soldiers sitting around their campfires in the winter of 1862–63 studying Latin, Greek, mathematics, and even Hebrew as they awaited the coming of the spring campaign.[9]

The second reason noted by Connelly was that the Army of Northern Virginia was fortunate enough to fight its battles near the capitals of the two nations and in a compact area close to the large population centers of the eastern seaboard. Most of that army's major battlefields are within a few hours' drive of the Richmond–New York megalopolis. "Everything's so *close* in Virginia," exclaimed an Arkansas Civil War buff after a 1984 visit to the eastern battlefields.

By contrast, the sites where the Army of Tennessee battled the Yankee invaders are scattered from Belmont, Missouri, to Bentonville, North Carolina, and from Perryville, Kentucky, to Jonesboro, Georgia. In the 1860s much of that vast area was sparsely populated, and even today a tourist has to go to considerable trouble to visit the sites of some of the western battles.

The nearness of the eastern battlefields to Richmond meant that the activities and personnel of the Army of Northern Virginia were closely and constantly scrutinized by both the Confederate government and the vigorous press of the capital. The success or failure of the Army of Northern Virginia, moreover, had a direct and immediate bearing on the government authorities whose families and official departments would have to flee the city if the eastern Rebel army could not defend it. Under these circumstances, it was natural for the government to pay a great deal of attention to the army in Virginia. Distance and sometimes poor communications as well as friction between some of the western commanders and the government isolated and insulated the Richmond bureaucrats from the effects of the Army of Tennessee's battles.

Third, observed Connelly, the Army of Tennessee did not possess a galaxy of glamorous generals to match those who fought in Virginia. Although such western leaders as the infamous, if colorful, Nathan Bedford Forrest and the brave and tragic Patrick R. Cleburne are worthy subjects for the time and attention of biographers and historians, most of the leaders of the western army were too dull or even repulsive to attract much attention. One does not find among the western generals a noble knight such as Lee or an eccentric genius to match Stonewall Jackson, and Joseph Wheeler and John Hunt Morgan are no rivals of Jeb Stuart as the dashing, gregarious Southern cavalier.

We have biographies of greater or lesser merit of all of the commanding generals and of almost all of the men who served as corps commanders in both armies. On the whole, the studies of the eastern leaders are better—a characteristic that stems more from the subjects than from the authors of those works. The high-ranking eastern generals are a more colorful lot of men who come alive in the pages of their biographies in a way that most of their lackluster western counterparts do not.[10]

Good biographies of generals in the Army of Northern Virginia do not stop with officers who served at the corps level. Many of the division and brigade commanders of the eastern army have had their life stories told in full-length studies. Books about the major generals and brigadier generals of the Army of Tennessee are unusual. We even have book-length biographies of such colonels and majors of the Virginia army as John Singleton Mosby, Sandie Pendleton, Henry King Burgwyn, Jr., and John Pelham. There are no comparable studies of lower-ranking officers in the Army of Tennessee and nothing to match the catalog of field grade officers in the Army of Northern Virginia compiled by Robert K. Krick or the Virginia Regimental Histories series published by H. E. Howard.[11]

Much of the biographical and personality problem regarding the generals of the Army of Tennessee is well illustrated by the case of the historian Grady McWhiney. He undertook to write a biography of General Braxton Bragg, the officer who commanded the Army of Tennessee for much of 1862 and 1863. McWhiney found his subject so nauseous that he abandoned the project after completing only the first of a projected two volumes. At last report he had turned the disgusting Bragg over to a graduate student.[12]

A fourth—and basic—reason why the Army of Tennessee has suffered relative neglect at the hands of both lay and professional students of the war, writes Connelly, was "a paucity of good historical writing." The rustic, relatively unlettered western army did not contain a glittering collection of diarists, memoirists, and other literati to rival those who served in the Virginia army. There was no E. Porter Alexander, G. Moxley Sorrel, Henry Kyd Douglas, John Esten Cooke, or George Cary Eggleston in the West and therefore no outstanding body of easily available source materials to serve as the basis for a history of the Army of Tennessee.[13]

Although Connelly does not deal with the subject, this same phenomenon, to a lesser degree, was also true of the Federals. Most of the Yankees who hailed from the literary, intellectual, and publishing centers of New York, New England, and Philadelphia fought in the East. Their interest in the war and its literature naturally centered on the area where they and their friends had served. As a result, Northern literature on the war is also skewed toward the East. When such writers dealt with their opponents, they wrote about the men they had faced in Virginia, Maryland, and Pennsylvania, not about the far-off and unknown Rebels in Tennessee and Georgia. Therefore, the Army of Northern Virginia was "the enemy" in much Northern writing about the war.

A large part of the manuscript source materials for a history of the Army of Tennessee was lost or destroyed, and what remains is widely scattered. A historian could write a good history of the Army of Northern Virginia from the manuscript sources in the Old Dominion; indeed, he or she would not have to travel west of the Blue Ridge. A similar work on the Army of Tennessee would necessitate travel to archives and libraries in at least half a dozen states.

Not surprisingly, this disparity in the volume of primary source

material has led to an abundance of writing about the war in
Virginia and, until recent times, a great paucity of studies of the
western battles. The eastern campaigns have been treated in
such detail that we have massive books about parts of some of the
battles in which the Army of Northern Virginia fought as well as
studies of many of the smaller engagements that took place in the
Old Dominion. One historian even wrote a 720-page book on
the sixth attempt by Union forces to capture Petersburg, Virginia,
29 September–2 October 1864. At that rate, extrapolated for the
entire 1861–65 period, a history of the war in the eastern theater
would fill a volume of 262,991 pages. By contrast, the western
battles have suffered relative neglect, and it has only been in
recent years that we have begun to see studies of many of them.[14]

The fifth and final reason for the neglect of the Army of
Tennessee, noted Connelly, was that "Southerners like a winner,
and the Army of Tennessee rarely won." In the decades long after
the war, aging Rebel veterans preferred to remember the battles
their side had won and to forget those they had lost. This selec-
tive amnesia was transmitted to their descendants, and the inherited disease has infected Confederate historiography well into
the late twentieth century. In 1984 an Arkansan came home from
the Old Dominion, proclaiming with all the ecstasy of a religious
pilgrim that he had "just returned from two weeks in the holy
land"—by which he meant Virginia's Civil War battlefields. Because virtually all of the major Rebel victories had been won in
battles fought in Virginia, the attention of white Southerners
came naturally to be focused on that theater of operations, and
the Rebel armies that had fought elsewhere tended to slip into
oblivion.[15]

This last reason, however, leads to other and deeper questions: Why was the Army of Northern Virginia so successful?
Why was the Army of Tennessee so often defeated? It is to these
problems that the remainder of this book is addressed.

CHAPTER TWO

Some Basic Factors

Although no historian has sought to cobble together an all-encompassing explanation for the military—and hence the historiographical—success of the Army of Northern Virginia as compared with the Army of Tennessee, several writers have put forth ideas that bear upon the problem. Some additional factors emerge from random reading in the original records of the war, and still others leap out from an 1860s map of the United States. What seems to have been the most important difference between the two great Rebel armies, however, is so clear that it went almost unnoticed during the war and has only rarely been considered since.

The contrasting features of the politics of secession in East and West was one obvious factor that worked to hamper the Confederates in the West even before the Army of Tennessee had formally come into existence. After Virginia's secession on 17 April 1861, the northern boundary of the Confederacy in the East was clearly marked, and the Rebel military commanders there knew what territory they had to defend. (It is true that some oversanguine secessionists believed that Maryland, where there was a great deal of prosecession sentiment, would join her sister slave states. The location of the national capital in Washington, D.C., however, and the resulting concentration of Northern military power there meant that any realistic possibility of the Old Line State's adherence to the Confederacy would have to await the negotiation of a peace settlement that gave her the opportunity to decide between the Union and the Confederacy.)[1]

In the West, the protracted struggles over Missouri and Kentucky created much uncertainty about just what area was in the Confederacy, and in so doing they hampered the western Rebels' military preparations. The problems raised by the enigmatic status of Kentucky proved to be especially harmful to the Army of Tennessee. They all but paralyzed the Confederates' western military operations for several crucial months in 1861 and hampered them for almost the entire war.

Torn between North and South, with strong emotional and economic ties to both sections and a long tradition of political compromise, Kentuckians sought escape from their dilemma in a policy of neutrality. Many of them innocently assumed that they could be a part of the United States and also remain neutral in a war in which their country was engaged and their state was on the frontier between the belligerent powers.

Despite its naiveté, the Kentuckians' position meant that any open, precipitate action by either side to establish its military presence might well push the state into the arms of the other. Throughout the war, Confederate authorities were appallingly ignorant of the political situation in Kentucky. To an alarming degree they were dependent for information upon the self-serving analyses of political refugees from the Bluegrass—men who had been forced to flee the state because their secessionist proclivities were contrary to the overwhelming public desire for peace, stability, and Union.

At first, the Confederate government, like its Northern counterpart, went through the motions of respecting Kentucky's uncommitted position even as the Rebels sought to lure the state into secession and established recruiting stations in northern Tennessee, where men from the Bluegrass State could easily enlist in the Southern army.

In the summer of 1861 Confederate President Jefferson Davis conferred "plenary powers" on Major General Leonidas Polk, the secessionist military commander in the Mississippi Valley. In early September Polk—obviously acting on his own initiative—violated Kentucky's neutrality by occupying the town of Columbus, on the Mississippi River about twenty miles north of the Bluegrass State's border with Tennessee. Soon the Rebels held an east-west line running across the southern part of Kentucky from Columbus on the west through Bowling Green to Cumberland Gap.

Polk's action touched off a flurry of confused correspondence among Confederate leaders, some of whom still hoped that Kentucky would remain neutral. Upon hearing of the invasion, Tennessee Governor Isham G. Harris wrote Polk that the general's action was "unfortunate as the President and myself are pledged to respect the neutrality of Kentucky." Harris also expressed the hope that Polk's troops would be "withdrawn instantly, unless their presence there is an absolute necessity." On 4 September Confederate Secretary of War Leroy P. Walker telegraphed Polk ordering the prompt withdrawal of the invading troops. On the same day, however, Davis—who, indeed, had little choice once his field commander had acted—overruled Walker and allowed Polk's men to stay in Kentucky. Instead of withdrawing, the Southerners proceeded to encourage the organization of a pro-Confederate state government while they justified the invasion as a preemptive step necessary to block the seizure of important points by Federal military forces.

Although Kentucky's neutral status was clearly dissolving in the late summer of 1861 and the state was drifting toward remaining in the Union, the Confederate general had placed his government in the awkward position of being the party that upset the status quo. For the Southern civil authorities to abandon control of so important a matter to the military was bad enough for their cause, but they soon made things even worse. They fell thoroughly under the bewitchment of the "Kentucky bloc," a group of political and military fugitives from the Bluegrass who continued to assert, despite overwhelming evidence to the contrary, that the vast majority of the people of Kentucky were panting to join the Confederacy and only awaited the coming of a Rebel army to throw off the shackles of Yankee despotism.

In December 1861 many Confederates convinced themselves that recent antislavery remarks by Federal Secretary of War Simon Cameron would drive Kentucky out of the Union. As late as the fall of 1864, the "liberation of Kentucky" was still a major goal of Confederate strategy in the West. The "Kentucky dream"—the desire to carry the Rebel banners to the southern bank of the Ohio—died hard, and it was always a millstone around the neck of the Army of Tennessee.[2]

The situation in Missouri was similar to that in Kentucky, although its impact on the Army of Tennessee was less direct and significant. Missouri's position, like that of Kentucky, was uncertain for much of 1861, and that uncertainty helped to prevent the formulation of a coherent Confederate policy for the area between the Mississippi and the Ozarks. A small minority of Missourians, including Governors Claiborne Jackson and Thomas C. Reynolds, sought throughout the war to drag their state into the Confederacy. Like their brethren in Kentucky, the Missouri Rebels organized a prosecessionist state government in exile, with its "permanent" capital located first in Camden, Arkansas, and then in Marshall, Texas. They pleaded with the authorities in Richmond to send troops to enable them to drive out the Yankees.

In the late summer of 1861 Confederate forces moving from Arkansas and Tennessee marched into the southern portion of Missouri and held the area until the following year. Missouri exiles yearned to return to their homes, and as late as the fall of 1864 a forlorn army of Trans-Mississippi Confederates marched into Missouri, hoping to reestablish their position in the state. So far as the Army of Tennessee was concerned, the hopeless Southern effort in Missouri served mostly to drain off manpower and resources that could have been better used in the more important area east of the Mississippi or at least in coordinated efforts by the Rebels on both sides of the great river.[3]

Probably the best example of the way the political situation in the West adversely affected Confederate strategy and hence the Army of Tennessee is to be seen in the defense of the lower Tennessee and Cumberland rivers in the early months of the war. The best place at which those rivers could have been closed to Yankee gunboats was in southwestern Kentucky, where the two streams are very close together and the terrain would best favor the defenders. Owing to their early desire to respect Kentucky's neutrality, however, the Southerners decided to construct their fortifications at a less well-situated point in Tennessee, a few miles upriver. By the time the Confederates violated Kentucky's neutral status, the plans to build the fortifications in Tennessee were so far advanced that it was decided to complete them. In other words, the Rebels marched into Kentucky early enough to ensure that the state would be driven into Federal arms but too late to derive any real military advantage from doing so.

NATURE, too, seemed to conspire against the Army of Tennessee, for geography, as well as secession politics, worked to help the eastern Rebels and to hamper those in the West. The Army of Northern Virginia was deployed to defend a narrow front east of the Allegheny Mountains. A line drawn across central Virginia from the Potomac River on the east, through Fredericksburg, to the Alleghenies on the west, is only about 160 miles long. The east-west distance along the Kentucky-Tennessee border from Cumberland Gap to the Mississippi River is over two and one-half times that length. In the first winter of the war, the western front was even wider because the commander of the western Confederates was then responsible for defending all the vast area between the Appalachians and the Ozark Mountains in western Missouri and Arkansas—a distance of almost 600 miles.

The Army of Northern Virginia campaigned in an area that was not only narrow but was also characterized by several terrain features favorable to its military operations. Many of the rivers in Virginia proved helpful to the eastern army. The Potomac, the Rappahannock, the Rapidan, the North Anna, and several lesser streams flow for at least part of their courses in relatively straight lines across Virginia more or less from west to east. They were parallel to the Army of Northern Virginia's lines of defense and perpendicular to the Federals' line of advance. Most of them could be forded at only a few points, and their high, difficult banks provided strong positions in which the Army of Northern

Virginia could await the advance of its enemy. The same rivers were obstacles across which the Federals had to transport their troops and supplies. The James River, which might have given the Yankees access to Richmond, was so situated that it could be closed by the strong Rebel fortifications that were built at Drewry's Bluff, a few miles below the capital.

By contrast, the Army of Tennessee operated for the first two and one-half years of the war in a region where the rivers both hampered its own movements and helped its enemy to advance. The Mississippi, the Cumberland, and especially the Tennessee were mighty streams that were dominated by Yankee gunboats from early in the war. They provided the Northerners with safe, convenient avenues to move easily and quickly deep into the geographical heartland of the Confederacy, and they ensured that advancing Yankee armies could readily be supplied and reinforced by boat. "The Mississippi River," writes the historian James M. McPherson, "was an arrow thrust into the heart of the Lower South."

The Mississippi flanked, and the Cumberland and the Tennessee broke, the defensive line that the Rebels established across southern Kentucky in late 1861. The same three rivers also constituted formidable obstacles to the east-west movement of Confederate troops along that line and across the Mississippi Valley.

The strategic problems that these rivers posed for the western Confederates did not end with the collapse of the Rebels' southern Kentucky line. The Mississippi provided an avenue for a Federal force moving northward from the Gulf of Mexico to operate against the left or rear of any Southern army in West Tennessee or Mississippi. Federal control of the Cumberland made it impossible for the Rebels to hold Nashville, the important political and manufacturing center of the western Confederacy. Once the lower Tennessee was open to Yankee gunboats— as it was after mid-February 1862—it was not possible for a large force of Confederates to operate for long north of that stream in the area southwest of Nashville. Loss of the lower Tennessee also weakened the Rebels' hold on northern Alabama and encouraged the rise of a hitherto dormant Unionism in that area.

In March 1862, after the debacle in which the Confederates lost their hold on Kentucky and much of Tennessee largely because of these rivers, a correspondent for the *Savannah Daily Republican* called the Tennessee "the heel of Achilles to our position in Kentucky and Tennessee." He could, with equal truth, have applied the same analogy to the Mississippi and the Cumberland.

In 1864 the fighting in the West shifted into North Georgia. Although the rivers there—the Oostanaula, the Etowah, the Chattahoochee, and lesser streams—were perpendicular to the Northern line of advance and were free from Yankee gunboats, they too proved disadvantageous to the Confederates. The serpentine meanderings of these streams greatly lengthened the river lines that the Rebels had to guard, and the "oxbows," or sharp bends in those rivers, created many places where sediments tended to settle; as a result, the water was shallow. A given stretch of a North Georgia river was likely therefore to provide a number of shallow fords at any of which the advancing Yankees could find an easy crossing and so outflank the Confederate defenses on the south bank.

In summary, the Virginia rivers favored the Southerners; the western waters helped the Yankees.[4]

THE Appalachian Mountains, which stretched from Pennsylvania to Alabama separating the Virginia theater of war from the West, also helped the eastern Confederates while hampering those in Tennessee. This great mountain range actually consists of three parts. Its eastern wall is the Blue Ridge Mountains; its western side, the Allegheny Mountains. In between these parallel mountain ridges is the Great Valley.

In Virginia the Valley, known locally as the Shenandoah Valley or the Valley of Virginia, runs from southwest to northeast. It offered the Rebels a covered route northward, pointing like a dagger at the heart of Yankeedom. A Confederate army that entered the Valley and marched to Harpers Ferry at its lower, or northern end, would be astride the Baltimore and Ohio Railroad, thus cutting one of the North's three major east-west rail lines. Such a force, with its flanks protected by the mountains on either side, would also be poised to threaten several important Northern cities. It would be fifty miles northwest of Washington, D.C., sixty-five miles west of Baltimore, and eighty-five miles southwest of Harrisburg, Pennsylvania, the capital of that important state and the site of crucial bridges that carried another of the North's east-west rail lines over the Susquehanna River. The Shenandoah Valley, in short, was a protected invasion route into the North. As Stonewall Jackson demonstrated in the spring of 1862, a Rebel army operating freely in the lower Valley could play havoc with Federal strategy in Virginia.

Because the Valley ran off to the southwest, it did not offer a comparable opportunity to the Yankees. A Federal army moving south through the Valley would be shunted off toward the isolated, desolate area of southwestern Virginia. Should a Union column penetrate as far up the Valley as Lexington, directly west of Richmond, it would be farther from the Rebel capital than if it had remained in Washington, and it would be without any rail or water connection with the North over which supplies could be brought to sustain it in an advance eastward.

In the West the military advantages offered by the Great Valley were reversed. A Federal force moving south through East Kentucky into the Valley would cut the vital Virginia and Tennessee Railroad, a part of one of the Rebels' three major east-west lines of communication and a rail line that one historian has called "probably the most vital [rail] artery in the Confederacy because it was the only direct link between Virginia and the West." The Yankees could then proceed down the Virginia and Tennessee Railroad and the Tennessee River through Knoxville and emerge at Chattanooga in the center of the Confederacy. Such a campaign would face formidable (probably insurmountable) logistical difficulties, but there were those in the North—not the least of whom was President Abraham Lincoln—who favored such an enterprise for both political and military reasons. The Confederates, therefore, had to be on guard to prevent such an invasion. By contrast, a Southern army moving up the East Tennessee Valley would be going into the barren area to the northeast, and every day's march would carry it farther away from cooperating Confederate forces in the central part of Tennessee.

THE history and politics of the Appalachian area as well as the region's geography proved to be heavy burdens for the Army of Tennessee. Opposition to secession was vigorous in the mountainous areas of the Upper South, where slavery had never been strongly entrenched, economic ties often bound the people to the North, and the inhabitants had long been underrepresented in state governments controlled by men from areas where the peculiar institution was a crucial part of both the society and the economy. Nowhere were these conditions more prevalent than in western Virginia and East Tennessee, and in both of those areas long-festering political resentment combined with strong Unionist sentiment to create opposition to secession and then resistance to Rebel rule.

In Virginia this movement led to the secession of several western counties from the Old Dominion and to the eventual formation of the new state of West Virginia. An attempt to create a government in East Tennessee that would withdraw from the Volunteer State and remain loyal to the Union was suppressed by Confederate military forces. Soon a vicious civil war within a civil war broke out in the mountains of East Tennessee as Unionist sympathizers battled Confederate troops and Rebel supporters, unattached guerrilla bands professing loyalty to neither side—or to either as the occasion demanded—raided and robbed everybody, and individuals took advantage of the chaos to settle old scores against their personal and political enemies.

The political turmoil in Virginia's far western counties was largely irrelevant to the Army of Northern Virginia. The area was on the periphery of the Old Dominion and the Confederacy, isolated from the strategically crucial regions of the state, and—except for the iron mills around Wheeling—it contained few important developed natural resources. It was not worth trying to hold onto, and it could be safely ignored until a postwar peace settlement decided its fate.

In East Tennessee the situation was quite different. The area was well within the Confederacy, and the Southerners had to maintain control of the Virginia and Tennessee Railroad to keep open the only direct line of communication between both the Rebel capital and the central South and the Mississippi Valley. East Tennessee was rich in lead, coal, and saltpeter (potassium nitrate). The region was also the location of the copper mines that produced more than 90 percent of the Confederacy's supply of that important metal.

The commanding general of the Army of Northern Virginia did not have to worry very much about developments in the isolated Unionist area over the Alleghenies far beyond his left flank. For the first two and a half years of the war the commanding general of the Army of Tennessee had to be concerned about the turmoil in the East Tennessee mountains lest it lead to the severing of a vital rail line, the loss of valuable natural resources, and the exposure of his army's right rear. To add insult to injury, the East Tennessee rail line drained off troops to guard its bridges, yards, and depots, but it rarely brought supplies or reinforcements to the Army of Tennessee.[5]

SEVERAL generations of historians have emphasized the vast demographic and economic advantages that the North enjoyed over the South. In the 1850s the states and territories that were to remain loyal to the Federal government experienced a population growth of 6,424,235 people, or 40.4 percent. In the same decade the states that were to form the Confederacy enjoyed a population increase of only 1,829,379 people—a growth of 25.1 percent. The area that supported the Union had a total population in 1860 of 22,339,921. In the same year the eleven soon-to-be Confederate states had a total population of 9,103,333, only

5,582,222 of whom were white. The seceding states contained only 29.3 percent of the population of the United States in 1860. The total number of people living in the three most populous Northern states—New York, Pennsylvania, and Ohio—exceeded the entire population of the Confederate states by 23,128 people. The inhabitants of New York and Pennsylvania alone outnumbered the white population of the Confederacy by 1,204,728.

The census officials defined the military-age population as white males between eighteen and forty-five years of age. Over 80 percent of the military-age population in 1860 lived in the states and territories that were to remain loyal to the Federal government. New York State's military population alone was three-fourths that of the entire Confederacy. New York, Massachusetts, and Vermont could have fielded an army that outnumbered the military-age population of the eleven Rebel states by 51,687 men. When those eastern Yankees needed to rest from the fatigues of war, they could have been replaced by a force from Illinois, Indiana, and Ohio that exceeded total Confederate strength by 35,662 men. Pennsylvania's half a million military-age men would have provided adequate replacements for any casualties, and the military-age men in the other sixteen Northern states could have gone about their normal business.

Federal superiority was not limited to a larger population. The North had approximately 110,000 manufacturing establishments; the Confederacy, 20,631. The North accounted for $1,560,575,277 worth of manufactured goods in 1860; the states that were to secede produced manufactured goods worth only $155,535,277. The value of goods manufactured in all eleven Confederate states in 1860 was 52.6 percent of the value of manufactured goods produced in Massachusetts alone in 1855. The free states had $43.73 per worker invested in manufacturing; the slave states only $13.25.

The eleven states of the Confederacy had in 1860 a total of 1,365 establishments that made shoes and boots; New York State had 2,277. Pennsylvania produced cotton goods valued at

$13,650,114 in 1860; the eleven Confederate states manufactured a total of only $8,145,067 worth of the same products. Massachusetts' $19,655,787 worth of woolen goods was almost ten times greater than the Confederate total of $1,995,324. Pennsylvania alone accounted for over half of the iron produced in the United States in 1860; Ohio was in second place; New Jersey in third. Ninety percent of the nation's money was in Northern banks in 1860.

Railroad mileage is another oft-cited example of Northern superiority. The Union states had, in 1860, a total of 21,506 miles of railroad; the Confederate states, 8,942 miles. Excluding Virginia, no two Confederate states had a combined rail mileage equal to that of any one of the top three Northern states—Ohio, New York, and Illinois. The trackage in those three states plus that in Pennsylvania exceeded the rail mileage in the entire Confederacy by more than 22 percent.

Union rail superiority took forms other than total miles of track. In 1860 American railroad shops manufactured a total of 470 locomotives; only 19 of them were made in the states that were to form the Confederacy. Virginia was the only Confederate state with a facility designed to manufacture locomotives; New Hampshire alone had four. Railroads from the North touched the Ohio River at twelve points opposite Kentucky; there were only three points at which the South had rail connections with the Bluegrass State.

Northern railroads were mostly standard gauge (four feet, eight and a half inches). They formed a rail system that permitted the movement of rolling stock directly from the tracks of one railroad to those of another. Many Confederate railroads lacked physical connection to other lines, and they had been built in at least three different gauges. One Rebel railroad had even been built in two different gauges (it was constructed from the ends toward the midpoint). Southerners, therefore, often found it necessary to unload passengers and freight from the trains of one rail line and load them onto those of another.[6]

These and similar data covering other facets of mid-nine-

The West, 1861–1865

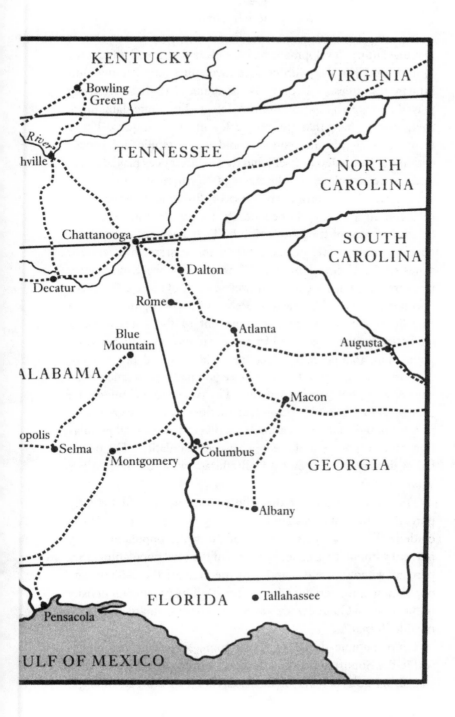

teenth-century development make it clear that the Confederacy fought the Civil War with comparatively limited economic and human resources, and there is no doubt that that inferiority played a major role in the Rebels' defeat. The same data, however, obscure facts that are more relevant to this inquiry. There were many significant economic and demographic differences within the Confederacy itself, and those differences played a role in the success enjoyed by the Army of Northern Virginia.

Historians have long been aware of differences between the relatively advanced level of economic development in the Upper South and that of the Lower South. They have not noticed the equally striking differences between the eastern and western states of the Cotton Kingdom. If one divides the Confederacy into three geographical areas, however, some of these differences become obvious. The eastern Rebel states—Virginia and the Carolinas—occupied only 19.2 percent of the Confederacy's land area. Yet they contained 37 percent of the new nation's white population, 36.2 percent of its total population, and 34.5 percent of its military-age population. The region had a population density of 22.1 people per square mile. The two central Confederate states—Georgia and Florida—had 15.1 percent of the area, 12.1 percent of the white population, 13.2 percent of the total population, and 11.9 percent of the military-age population. The population density of the central Confederacy was 10.2 people per square mile.

The western states of the Confederacy accounted for 65.7 percent of the country's land area (31.3 percent if Texas is excluded). They had 50.1 percent of the white population (43.3 percent without Texas), 50.2 percent of the total population (48.7 percent without Texas), and 53.6 percent of the military-age population (44.9 percent without Texas). The population density of the western Confederacy was 8.3 people per square mile (14.9 outside Texas).[7]

The economic data also reveal some important differences within the Southern nation. The three eastern Rebel states had a staggering 40.8 percent of the Confederacy's railroad mileage.

The states of the central South had 20.2 percent of the Rebels' rail mileage, and the western states only 39 percent (35.6 percent excluding Texas). In the eastern Confederacy there was one mile of railroad for every 40.8 square miles of area and for every 903 people. In the central states, one mile of track existed for every 65.1 square miles and for every 664 people. In the western states of Rebeldom, there was one mile of railroad for every 146.3 square miles (every 76.4 square miles excluding Texas) and one mile of track to every 1,322 people (1,259 not counting Texas).

Manufacturing statistics tell a similar story. The three eastern Confederate states contained 10,304 (49.9 percent) of the new nation's manufacturing establishments in 1860 and produced $75,950,017 (48.8 percent) of its $155,535,277 worth of manufactured products. The central Confederacy's 2,075 manufacturing establishments (10.1 percent of the total) made $19,373,524 (12.5 percent) of the country's manufactured goods. The western states had 8,252 manufacturing facilities (40 percent of the total; 7,269 and 35.2 percent without Texas). They produced $60,211,736 worth of manufactured goods (38.7 percent of the total; $53,634,534 and 33.8 percent excluding Texas).

Nowhere in the Confederacy was antebellum economic development as advanced as in Virginia, where, for almost half a century, the state government, acting through its Board of Public Works, had energetically fostered the growth of transportation and economic facilities. Virginia had more white inhabitants (1,105,453), more slaves (490,865), and more military-age white males (196,587) than did any other Rebel state. Virginia's 1,771 miles of railroad gave her more trackage than any of her seceding sisters. Indeed, 19.8 percent of the Confederacy's entire railroad mileage was within her borders, and her one mile of track for every 36.7 square miles of area was second only to South Carolina's as the best ratio in the South.

There are no available data on the rolling stock of the Confederate railroads, but Virginia's lines were well equipped with locomotives and cars. Angus Johnston, the historian of the Old Dominion's Civil War railroads, wrote: "It appears that the motive power of Virginia railroads in 1861 was as good as could be found anywhere in the United States."

Virginia alone produced more than 32.5 percent of the Confederacy's manufactured goods. Her factories turned out more cotton goods, more woolen goods, more agricultural implements, and more of many other items than did the factories of any other Confederate state. Her production of bar, sheet, and railroad iron was more than three times greater than that of second-place Tennessee. Indeed, Virginia's iron production had grown by 194 percent in the 1850s while Tennessee's had declined by 30.8 percent. Virginia's 5,385 manufacturing establishments, the state's $26,935,560 of capital invested in manufacturing, and its $50,652,124 worth of manufactured goods dwarfed the contributions of any other Rebel state. Henrico County (Richmond) produced more manufactured goods than did Alabama, Arkansas, Florida, Mississippi, South Carolina, or Texas. Had Henrico County been a state, it would have ranked sixth among the then twelve Rebel states in the value of its industrial output, and the rest of Virginia would still have produced more than twice as many manufactured goods (measured by value) as Tennessee.

The economic superiority of the eastern Rebel states did not end with their greater industrial plant. Virginia's infrastructure was far better situated for military purposes than was that of any other Southern state. Except for the Baltimore and Ohio running across the northern part of what is now West Virginia and two short railroads along the Potomac River, Virginia's rail lines were concentrated east of the Blue Ridge, pretty much in the central portion of what is now the state of Virginia. It was within that area that the Army of Northern Virginia fought most of its battles, and within that area it had the support of a rail network over which troops and supplies could be transported.

Probably the most important rail advantage for an army operating in the Old Dominion, however, was that the state's railroads formed what was, by Confederate standards, a genuine rail system. All of the Confederate railroads in Virginia north of Richmond in the east and Lynchburg in the west were of standard gauge, and at Hanover Junction, Charlottesville, Gordonsville, and Manassas Junction their tracks were physically joined so that trains could pass from one rail line to another without having to unload. For at least part of the war there were also interchanges in Richmond when tracks were laid through some of the city's streets. The interchanges and common gauge meant that troops moving within the Old Dominion and troops and supplies from the Deep South could be transported quickly by rail to their Virginia destinations without the necessity of unloading from one train, moving across town to another railroad station, and loading onto another train to continue the journey.

The Army of Tennessee almost always had rail transportation to and from its area of operations, but only twice did it enjoy something even approaching a rail system in its immediate vicinity. In the early months of the war the railroads of West Tennessee offered the western Rebels some of the same facility for transportation that the Army of Northern Virginia enjoyed for almost the entire war. West Tennessee, however, was lost to the South early in 1862, in large part because of the geographical factors discussed above. For a few weeks during the fighting around Atlanta in the summer of 1864, the Army of Tennessee was able to use the local railroads to facilitate some of its movements.

The Rebels' western railroads formed a system of sorts by which one could make, say, a journey around the western Confederacy from Memphis to Chattanooga and then on through Atlanta, Montgomery, Mobile, and Corinth back to Memphis. This "system," however, was spread over so great an area that it was of little immediate use to the Army of Tennessee, and it involved a long journey with several changes of railroads. Such travel was not comparable to the ease with which a Virginian could go from Richmond to Lynchburg, to Gordonsville, and back to Richmond.

Jefferson Davis's February 1861, journey as Rebel president-elect from his Mississippi home to his inauguration in Mont-

gomery, Alabama, typified the odyssey that was often synonymous with rail travel in the western states of the Confederacy.
Davis had to travel from Jackson, Mississippi, north to Grand
Junction, Tennessee (at which point he was outside the boundaries of the then Confederate States), east to Chattanooga, south
to Atlanta, and then southwest through Columbus to Montgomery. His rail journey covered more than 700 miles. The direct
distance from Jackson to Montgomery is about 250 miles. The
leg of Davis's trip from Grand Junction to Chattanooga took him
along what was to be the Confederacy's northernmost east-west
rail line. That line was about 200 miles south of the position held
by the Army of Tennessee in the winter of 1861–62—far too
distant to be of any practical day-to-day use to the Rebels—and
the line was exposed at several points to Federals moving by boat
along the Tennessee River.

Virtually all of the major western railroads were long point-to-
point lines running from, for example, New Orleans to Memphis
or Mobile to Montgomery. Often a western rail journey had to be
broken because of an unbridged body of water (Mobile Bay; the
Tombigbee River at Demopolis, Alabama), because the gauges
of railroads were different (Montgomery, Alabama; Columbus,
Georgia), or because a long gap existed between the end of one
railroad and the beginning of another (Selma to Montgomery,
Alabama; Blue Mountain, Alabama, to Rome, Georgia).

Often Confederate railroads in both East and West fell into the
hands of the Yankees for longer or shorter periods of time or
were damaged in military operations or by rock slides, floods,
and so on, and both Rebel armies found that their freedom of
maneuver was sometimes limited by the necessity of protecting
their rail communications. The point is that, on balance, the
Virginia rail lines were far more useful to the Army of Northern
Virginia than the western railroads were to the Army of Tennessee. Virginia's infrastructure also included what was, by Confederate standards, a well-developed road network and the important James River Canal.[8]

The Army of Northern Virginia, therefore, fought to defend a relatively small area and drew upon the much more highly developed economic resources of Virginia and the Carolinas as well as upon much of the production of Georgia, Florida, and even of Tennessee to sustain itself. The Army of Tennessee had to protect a vast region and never had comparable economic support or anything even approaching equal access to the Confederacy's economic resources. After the first year of the war, this difference became even more pronounced because vast areas of Tennessee and Louisiana—the Confederacy's second and fifth most economically developed states—were permanently lost to the Rebels.[9]

POLITICS, geography, history, and economics were all preexisting factors that favored the Army of Northern Virginia over its western counterpart. No human could have done anything to alter the facts of their existence once the war had started—although different policies by the Confederate government could have lessened their deleterious effect on the Army of Tennessee.

After the fighting began, popular ideas as well as military and political decisions made by generals and other officials on both sides began to come into play. Many of these ideas and decisions had the unintended side effect of helping one of the two major Confederate armies while hampering the other.

CHAPTER THREE

The Yankee Influence

O ne of the more ludicrous aspects of much of the writing on the American Civil War is the intense zealousness with which some of those who seek to explain some facet of the conflict have managed to focus their attention on only one side of this or that disputed point. This tendency is well illustrated by some of the writings that have been produced in an effort to resolve the perennial conundrum of why the Army of Northern Virginia went down to defeat in the July 1863 Battle of Gettysburg. Because Gettysburg has often been regarded as the decisive battle of the war, the answer to the question of why it ended as it did has been assumed to be very important to an understanding of the outcome of the conflict.

For decades writers poured out a steady stream of books and articles in which they argued that this or that action—or failure to act—by some Rebel general had determined the outcome of the battle and, by extension, of the war. Many writers hypothesized that the Confederate defeat at Gettysburg was entirely the fault of Major General James Ewell Brown (Jeb) Stuart, commander of the cavalry of the Army of Northern Virginia. Stuart's fragile ego and his glowing prestige, they argue, had been badly bruised in June 1863, when he had performed less than brilliantly in the great clash of cavalry at Brandy Station. Consequently, during the Gettysburg Campaign, Stuart took advantage of discretionary orders to ride off in an effort to redeem himself by chasing glory in the form of Yankee supply wagons when he should have been scouting the area and providing General Lee with timely and accurate intelligence on the movements and strength of the Federals. Lacking such information, the Army of

Northern Virginia blindly stumbled into the battle at Gettysburg, ignorant of its foe's strength, location, capabilities, and intent.

Other writers have heaped blame on the shoulders of Lieutenant General Richard S. Ewell, commander of the Second Corps of the army. Many believe that Ewell's recent marriage to the widow Brown ("My wife, Mrs. Brown," he is said once to have remarked as he introduced her) may have combined with the amputation of his leg following an 1862 wound to upset his psychological equilibrium to such an extent that he was unwilling or unable to make necessary decisions. Because Ewell did not press his attack on the first day of the battle, it is alleged, the Southerners missed an excellent opportunity to gain possession of crucial terrain. Over the next two days many Rebels would be killed or wounded in an unsuccessful effort to occupy the ground that Ewell could easily have seized on the battle's first day. Perhaps, however, it was not all Ewell's fault. Some students of the battle place the responsibility on Major General Jubal A. Early, one of Ewell's division commanders, who may have urged caution upon and exercised dominance over his indecisive superior.

If the hidden hand of Early did not bring about the Confederate defeat at Gettysburg, then perhaps the blame lies at the door of Lieutenant General James Longstreet, commander of the First Corps. The onus for the Rebel defeat at Gettysburg has, in fact, been dumped on Longstreet far more often than on any other Confederate general. Many of his critics have asserted that the commander of the First Corps dawdled on the second day of the battle when he should have been hurrying his men into position for an attack on the far left end of the Union line. Other writers have claimed that Longstreet threw away an excellent opportunity to win the battle that day when he refused to take his subordinates' advice to swing around the left end of the Federal position and attack the Yankee flank and rear. On the third day, many writers have alleged, Longstreet "sulked" and "pouted," and his efforts were less than enthusiastic because Lee had rejected his ideas about the best course for the Confederates to follow. Consequently, Longstreet again delayed in his preparations, and the great Rebel attack failed.

Some students of the battle have faulted Major General George E. Pickett for not personally leading the great charge that bears his name. Had Pickett, mounted and with a flashing sword in hand, galloped across the battlefield at the head of his charging brigades, who can doubt that Rebel spunk would have carried the day? Instead of gloriously leading his men in the charge, Pickett remained behind his advancing troops, where he could ascertain what was happening and supervise the overall development of the attack.

Perhaps the commander of Lee's Third Corps, Lieutenant General Ambrose Powell Hill, was responsible for the battle's outcome. Hill's "rashness" brought on the engagement on 1 July, when he sent some of his men to tangle with the Federals west of Gettysburg. Then, having precipitated the great battle, Hill spent the next several days doing very little. Hill, wrote one historian, "seemed in one of his funks, mad at someone, probably Lee." Maybe Hill's health was to blame. He was new as a corps commander, and the unaccustomed responsibility of directing so large a command in battle may have overwhelmed him and triggered some psychosomatic disorder. Perhaps, as Russell P. Green has suggested, Hill suffered from a depressive illness inherited from his mother (a depressive gene on the X-chromosome). At Gettysburg, Green thinks, he was "ineffective, often incompetent," because he was then in one of his genetically induced "low moods." William W. Hassler, who published a biography of Hill in 1957, thought that the general suffered from chronic malaria. More likely, as Hill's most recent biographer, James I. Robertson, Jr., convincingly argues, the general was then beginning the final stages of a bout with prostatitis, the result of his having contracted gonorrhea in 1844 when he was a cadet at West Point. It is probable that the disease would have brought about Hill's death in 1865 or 1866 if a Yankee bullet had not put him out of his misery on 2 April 1865.

A few historians of the battle have even had the temerity to criticize Lee himself. "Marse Robert," they claim, had whipped the Yankees so often and with such ease that, in the summer of 1863, he was overconfident. A contempt for his opponent and an exaggerated belief in the prowess of his own army led Lee to make careless tactical mistakes that cost him victory in the battle. Lee, it is also said, was a kind, overly considerate man who was unwilling to ride herd on his sometimes undisciplined staff and his headstrong and rambunctious subordinates to ensure that they carried out his orders. Other students of the battle, somewhat more charitably, attribute Lee's July 1863 ineptness to illness—the great Confederate commander may have had a touch of indigestion, or diarrhea, or maybe a mild heart attack.

It has even been suggested—perhaps facetiously—that the blame lies on the shoulders of Stonewall Jackson. If "Old Jack" had not gotten himself shot at Chancellorsville, surely the Confederacy would have won its independence at Gettysburg.

All of these explanations have two things in common. First, each of them places responsibility for the outcome of the battle solely and squarely on the back of a particular Confederate general. Second, and more relevant, all of them ignore completely a significant feature of Gettysburg—the presence on the battlefield of Major General George G. Meade and some ninety thousand officers and men of the Yankee Army of the Potomac, whose conduct in early July 1863 probably had some bearing on the outcome of the struggle around the little Pennsylvania town.

At Gettysburg, as the historian Edwin B. Coddington made clear in his fine, if somewhat tiresome, book *The Gettysburg Campaign: A Study in Command,* Meade simply outgeneraled Lee and the common soldiers of the Union army rose to heights of courage, sacrifice, and devotion that they had never reached before and never surpassed afterward. In summary, the Northerners were also involved at Gettysburg, and their presence had some impact on the battle there and on the course of the war. In at least three ways, moreover, the Yankees also affected the differing fortunes of the Army of Tennessee and the Army of Northern Virginia.[1]

THE different quality of the generals who led the Union forces in the East and in the West was one way the Federals contributed—quite by accident—to the unequal fortunes of the two main Confederate armies. For almost the entire war the western Rebels found themselves opposed by Federal forces led by Major Generals William T. Sherman and George H. Thomas. Sherman was a military intellectual given to thinking deeply about the warfare that he saw going on about him. He was probably the most creative and intuitively brilliant of all the high-ranking Civil War generals. Thomas, although by birth a Virginian, was the Federal army's most thorough, consistent, and dependable field commander. Together Sherman and Thomas made a very formidable combination leading the western Yankees. Ironically, both had begun their Civil War service in the Virginia theater, where they had held minor commands before being transferred to the West.

For much of the war the western Confederates also had to do battle against Union troops who were led or directed by such able commanders as Henry W. Halleck, William S. Rosecrans, Ulysses S. Grant, Philip H. Sheridan, James B. McPherson, and John M. Schofield. From its first battle at Belmont, Missouri, on 7 November 1861, to its surrender on 26 April 1865 at Bennett's Farm near Durham Station, North Carolina, the Army of Tennessee was always opposed by at least one of these outstanding generals. In the crucial battles fought around Chattanooga in late November 1863, General Braxton Bragg's western Rebels were routed by a force of Yankees commanded by Grant, with Sherman and Thomas acting as two of his chief lieutenants and Sheridan commanding one of his divisions. "No wonder there was so little left of Braxton Bragg," wrote the historian John Fiske. The Army of Northern Virginia, by contrast, had the good fortune to cut its military teeth on a collection of Yankee commanders who were of somewhat less than mediocre ability.[2]

The Yankee Influence

To command a Civil War army successfully, a general had to have at least four elements working in his favor. First, he had to have the technical knowledge to administer his army, to keep it trained and supplied, and to plan and execute its movements. Much of the nitty-gritty of this work, of course, was done by the general's staff and by his subordinate commanders under the general's supervision. Of the four prerequisites, this was the most easily acquired, and very few officers who lacked it became army commanders. Second, he needed the confidence, or at least the obedience, of the officers and men under his command. Third, a successful commander must have had enough self-confidence, enough faith in his own judgment, enough ruthlessness, and enough moral courage to execute the plans he devised and to order thousands of men—including, quite probably, many of his friends and even relatives—to their deaths to achieve his objectives.

Finally, and most important, there must have been cooperation between the government and its military commander. The successful general had to have the confidence of and adequate support from his civilian superiors in the government—the president and the secretary of war. Under the form of government that existed in both the Confederacy and the Union, an army commander could not allow himself to become publicly identified as an aspirant for the chief executive's office, an opponent of the government, or a stalking-horse for the government's political enemies. All four of these conditions were always met by the more successful Yankee generals in the West. For the first two and a half years of the war at least one of them was missing completely from the Federal command structure in the East.

The first Northerner to command the Federal forces in Virginia was Brigadier General Irvin McDowell, a plump native of Ohio and an 1838 graduate of the United States Military Academy, who had also undertaken additional study at French military schools. McDowell's political friends secured a brigadier generalship for him in 1861 even though his entire antebellum military career had been spent as a staff officer and he had never commanded even so much as a company in the field. Warren W. Hassler, who made a study of the Union commanders in Virginia, concluded that McDowell was "somewhat pompous and punctilious." Hassler also noted that McDowell "had none of those traits of personal magnetism which have often made inferior generals very popular with the rank and file" and that he "lacked real confidence in himself and in his ability to win." Kenneth P. Williams, another historian of the Federal army, commenting on McDowell's lack of assertiveness, observed that he "could not quite realize that he had [a general's] stars on his shoulders." The historian William C. Davis noted that McDowell was characterized by "a certain lack of humor coupled with a stiff formality or aloofness that separated him automatically from his subordinates and superiors." He was "a bad listener" and was "sometimes rude." T. Harry Williams wrote that he "was impulsive and often censorious and dogmatic; hence he offended many people. There was a large amount of the prig in him. . . . He was oppressed with his difficulties." In summary, McDowell was "unfitted by training and experience for army command." Unfortunately for McDowell, he received little cooperation from several of the other Northern generals, who either did not like him or who resented his elevation to army command. At the First Battle of Manassas on 21 July 1861 he "lost effective control of the battle," and his "timidity" and "lack of decision and confidence in his own judgment" nullified what was basically a sound battle plan and helped to bring about the eventual defeat and rout of his army.[3]

McDowell's successor, Major General George B. McClellan, was probably the most controversial Union general of the war. A Pennsylvanian by birth and a member of the West Point Class of 1846, McClellan enjoyed distinction before the Civil War as both an army officer and a civil engineer. Some minor successes in western Virginia early in the war led to his appointment in late July 1861 to command the Army of the Potomac.

In his ability to organize and train an army, win its loyalty, and prepare it for battle, McClellan was among the very best of Civil

War generals. Once he moved his forces out to meet the enemy, however, McClellan's considerable liabilities began to weigh in the scale. He had much too high an opinion of himself. In Hassler's words, "He believed that he was the chosen instrument of the Almighty to save the Union, and [he] acted accordingly." Kenneth P. Williams noted that McClellan was characterized by "great vanity" and a "lack of balance" and that he had an "intolerable and somewhat childish habit of saying that disaster would not be his fault if his wishes were not granted."

McClellan was also burdened by his "tendency to be a perfectionist" in a war in which things rarely went perfectly—especially for Yankee commanders in Virginia. McClellan was also petty. In the midst of a great campaign, noted Kenneth P. Williams, he "had time to listen to gossip and indulge in personal pique." Bruce Catton wrote of McClellan that "the ability to take quick, decisive action had been left out of his makeup."

Nor did McClellan have much ability to understand the human environment in which he found himself. Some idea of his grasp of the military and political situation he faced can be seen in his evaluation of his chief opponent and his civilian superiors. Lee, McClellan wrote in 1862, was "cautious and weak under grave responsibility . . . wanting in moral firmness when pressed by heavy responsibility . . . likely to be timid and irresolute in action." Of his civilian commander in chief McClellan wrote (privately) that Abraham Lincoln "was an old stick, and of pretty poor timber at that." In his personal correspondence he called Secretary of War Edwin M. Stanton an "unmitigated scoundrel."

McClellan's greatest liability as commander of the Army of the Potomac, however, had nothing to do with his many undesirable personal characteristics or with his lack of a clear understanding of his foe or of his place in the Federal hierarchy. McClellan was a very cautious and conservative man. Like many cautious and conservative Northerners, he hoped that the Civil War could be fought and won quickly and the Union preserved without introducing widespread changes into American society. Because of his conservatism, McClellan approached the conflict with an attitude that was fundamentally different from that of the Radical Republican politicians who hoped to use the opportunity presented by the war to strike at the institution of slavery. McClellan's political friends, for whom he sometimes staged elaborate dinners while he commanded the army, were the political enemies of the Lincoln administration. Like most regular army officers, McClellan was a Democrat—"a loud" Democrat, writes one historian—and he "intemperately declared more than once his lack of sympathy with the administration on political matters." As time went on, McClellan came to be viewed by his fellow Democrats as their hero and the hope of their party.

The combination of an arrogant, thin-skinned, cautious, conservative Democrat commanding the most prominent field army of a government headed by a very politically sensitive Republican chief executive who wanted his generals to show fight and who was under mounting pressure from the Radical wing of his own party to strike at slavery proved to be too much for either Lincoln or McClellan to handle.

Had McClellan been able to win victories, he would certainly have remained in command of the Federal forces in Virginia and probably would have been elected president in 1864 or 1868. As it was, his cautious temperament militated against the vigorous waging of victorious battles, and his career was a series of missed opportunities. In the spring of 1862 McClellan moved slowly to put his army below Richmond on the peninsula formed by the James and York rivers. As he advanced to within sight of the Rebel capital, McClellan found that reinforcements originally intended for his army were being used to meet an emergency elsewhere. Overawed by the Confederates in his front and erroneously believing his army to be outnumbered by his opponents, McClellan retreated when he was attacked and began to complain of the niggardly treatment that he and his army had received at the hands of the Lincoln administration. He convinced himself that many Republican politicians in the government wanted him to be defeated so that the war would continue and they could use it as a means to advance their own political goals.

McClellan's correspondence soon reflected the unfortunate personality traits that went a long way toward nullifying whatever military ability he had. "At times," writes Hassler, "he showed an obtuseness and a lack of tact in dealing with politicians and with his civilian superiors." He refused to take the civilian authorities into his confidence and practically accused them of trying to wreck his army. Not surprisingly, McClellan soon became "the chief target for slander, abuse, and interference" by the Radical Republicans, whose center of power was in Congress. McClellan's prominence as the probable 1864 Democratic presidential nominee did nothing to enhance his rapport with either the Radicals or President Lincoln. Kenneth P. Williams wrote that "McClellan was not a real general. McClellan was not even a disciplined, truthful soldier. McClellan was merely an attractive but vain and unstable man, with considerable military knowledge, who sat a horse well and wanted to be President."[4]

The third Federal commander in Virginia was Kentucky-born Major General John Pope, an 1842 graduate of the Military Academy, who had enjoyed some military success in the Mississippi Valley before he was placed in command in Virginia in the summer of 1862. Pope was an aggressive, bold commander. He had great confidence in and enthusiasm for himself, but many of his contemporaries viewed him as "a humbug," "a bag of wind," "a braggart," "a liar," "bombastic," "an ass," and "untruthful and wholly unreliable." Hassler comments that Pope combined "an impetuous nature" with "a lack of grasp of military probabilities"—a fatal combination of flaws for a Yankee general operating in Virginia. He was, writes Hassler, "an obnoxious character . . . really one of the most pathetic figures of the Civil War on the Federal side." In August 1862, when he opposed Lee in the campaign that ended with the rout of the Union army at Second Manassas, Pope "was in a blue funk as to what was going on." In the wake of his humiliating defeat, Pope was shipped off to Minnesota to chase Indians.[5]

After Pope's departure, McClellan was restored to command, and he led the Army of the Potomac during the Sharpsburg

(Antietam) Campaign. In the fall of 1862, however, McClellan performed no more satisfactorily than he had done in the preceding spring, and on 7 November 1862 he was replaced by Major General Ambrose E. Burnside. A native of Indiana and an 1847 Military Academy graduate, Burnside had acquired a greatly inflated reputation early in the Civil War when he won a few minor victories along the North Carolina coast. He was an easygoing man, and he had not performed well as a corps commander in the Army of the Potomac. Many of the officers and men seem not to have had any confidence in him. Even worse, Burnside himself "knew that he was incompetent to command such a host" as the Army of the Potomac.

Historians have not been kind to Burnside. Hassler observes that, at the time he was placed in command of the army, Burnside "was probably the most incompetent of all the general officers then serving with the Army of the Potomac, although Washington was apparently largely ignorant of the low opinion held of him by his brother officers." T. Harry Williams wrote that "there . . . [was] not much behind his showy front. . . . He did not have the brains to command a large army. . . . [He was] a man of incompetence." Emory M. Thomas notes that, when appointed to head the army, Burnside was reported to have said, "I am not fit to command this army." "Having made the statement," writes Thomas, "Burnside then proceeded to prove its validity." Charles Fair, who wrote a delightful chronicle of military stupidity entitled *From the Jaws of Victory*, dedicated his book to Burnside, whom he called "one of the greatest in a tradition still very much alive."

When he repeatedly sent his men into hopeless headlong assaults against the Army of Northern Virginia's very strong position at Fredericksburg in December 1862, Burnside displayed his "inflexible mind rigidly adhering to his preconceptions," as well as "a lack of practical imagination." He "just seemed to lose all tactical judgment and perception when he could not break through the enemy's lines. . . . [He] became more and more appalled, lost his ability to think clearly, and could only keep repeating his original ideas." Only the pleas of loyal subordinates prevented him from leading a suicide charge against the Rebels. Of Burnside's leadership at Fredericksburg, Fair asks, "Can he really have been *that* stupid?"

Soon after the crushing defeat at Fredericksburg, Burnside's troops booed him, and there were mutterings that they would refuse to fight again under his command. Some of his generals wrote to President Lincoln criticizing Burnside's plans, and two of the generals went personally to the White House and told the chief executive that their commander was leading the army to yet another disaster. Unlike many defeated generals, however, Burnside did exhibit a saving grace: he "was man enough to acknowledge his incompetency to handle such a massive host and to admit the wisdom of Lincoln in removing him from command."[6]

When Burnside surrendered command of the Army of the Potomac, he was replaced by Massachusetts-born Major General Joseph Hooker, an 1837 West Point graduate. Although a competent combat leader at the division and corps level and a fine administrator who rebuilt the army's tone, discipline, and morale, Hooker was not a felicitous choice as an army commander. Several of those who knew him noted that his complexion was habitually "flushed," and many of them speculated that the condition may have been caused by his well-known "fondness for drink." Hooker was also known to have had a "glad eye for ladies of easy virtue."

The general was also a man of flexible principles, who "had done a flip-flop" from his early wartime conservatism to radicalism to secure political support from that wing of the Republican party. He "had a penchant for gossip," and his behind-the-back criticism of Burnside had helped to undermine that unfortunate general. Hooker "never wearied of thumping his own chest and expounding on his own fancied talents as an army commander." He "was incapable of sustained mental concentration of a high order" and "crippled by his lack of imagination." With the exception of McClellan, he got along worse with President Lincoln than did any other high-ranking Federal general.

In the spring of 1863 Hooker devised a brilliant plan to strike at Lee's army in the heavily wooded area west of Fredericksburg. Moving quickly, the Federal commander placed his troops in what appeared to be an excellent position to trap Lee's men or force them to retreat. At the crucial moment, however, Hooker seemed to lose his nerve. Kenneth P. Williams wrote that "heavy responsibility, fatigue and nervous exhaustion had stripped away the mask of personal bravery, ready confidence, and boastfulness which he had always worn, and left the real Joe Hooker—unprepared by previous contemplation and humble self-examination for the terrible ordeal of a commanding general opposed by a very able adversary, who had several times been through that trial."

While Hooker hesitated, Lee seized the initiative and sent Stonewall Jackson marching around the right flank of the Union army. Jackson's crunching attack on the Yankee right at Chancellorsville wrecked Hooker's plan and a portion of his army. Hooker himself "ruined everything" by issuing unwise orders, and soon his beaten army was forced to withdraw to the position it had held when the campaign began. As "bad as Burnside was," writes one student of military history, "Hooker, as he showed at Chancellorsville. . . . was, if anything, worse, attempting more and taking far greater risks before he lost his nerve and his wits and 16,792 men."

Hooker's problems at Chancellorsville may have stemmed from a "loss of nerve" or from his "lack of ability to visualize, direct, and co-ordinate the changing positions and combinations of large bodies of troops by reports." Perhaps, as Hassler suggests, Hooker's decision not to "continue his usual drinking" during the campaign was the source of his difficulty. On the other hand, a careful modern student of the battle believes that Hooker was drunk at Chancellorsville. Whatever the reason, and whether Hooker was drunk or sober, his scalp joined those of McDowell, McClellan, Pope, and Burnside in the Army of Northern Virginia's trophy room.[7]

The Yankee Influence

Major General George G. Meade, who replaced Hooker on 28 June 1863, had been born to American parents in Spain and graduated from West Point in 1835. Meade was a man whose character was "essentially fine and useful." He "impressed people as having a great deal of brains and a well-balanced mind." He was also "a master of logistics" and a man of moral courage and great physical bravery. Perhaps best of all, he was completely apolitical and independent of the numerous cliques that existed within the army. Meade was not, however, an aggressive commander, and he was "nervous, dyspeptic, and irascible," as well as being "quite touchy" and "totally devoid of charisma." He "allowed responsibility to weigh him down," and he was not a general who was able to "inspire his soldiers with his personality, although he was . . . of commanding presence."

For all his drawbacks, Meade was by far the best commander the Army of the Potomac ever had. Hassler calls him "a sound though by no means a great commander." Meade directed the Army of the Potomac until the end of the war, although in 1864 and 1865 he operated under the direct supervision of Lieutenant General Ulysses S. Grant, who had been placed in command of all the Federal military forces and who elected to keep the eastern Yankee army under his own close control.[8]

It was thus not until mid-1863 that the Federals on the eastern front had a reasonably stable and competent leader to pit against Lee. Even then, it was not until the following spring—when Grant and Sheridan arrived in Virginia (the latter to assume command of the eastern cavalry)—that the Army of Northern Virginia had to face even some of the drive, tenacity, and leadership with which the Army of Tennessee had been contending from the beginning of the war. By the time Grant arrived in the East, Lee had lost Jackson and his army had passed its peak. Until some historian puts the question to a computer, we shall not know what would have happened if a Rebel army commanded by Lee, Longstreet, Jackson, and Stuart had faced a Union force under Grant, Sherman, Thomas, and Sheridan.

A second way in which Northern factors helped to explain the different fortunes of the two great Rebel armies is described and analyzed in the thesis put forward by Michael C. C. Adams in his interesting work *Our Masters the Rebels*. The book carries as its provocative subtitle *A Speculation on Union Military Failure in the East, 1861–1865*.

Adams's work is an examination of several ideas about their nation and about warfare that were held by many Americans in the mid-nineteenth century. Americans believed, among other things, that their country had been peopled by two distinct types (or "races") of Englishmen. Settlers who came to Virginia were believed to have been members of the English aristocracy—the "Cavaliers," in the language of the seventeenth century. They were regarded as the descendants of the Norman aristocrats who had followed William the Conqueror across the Channel in 1066 and whose families had ruled England for half a millennium. Those Englishmen who migrated to Massachusetts, on the other hand, were believed to have been of Saxon ancestry and to have come from the lower socioeconomic classes of the British Isles— the very people who had been defeated and conquered by the aristocratic, chivalrous Norman knights.

On this erroneous historical foundation nineteenth-century Americans erected a series of myths that were profoundly to influence the way the Civil War was conducted. Aristocratic Southern cavaliers, it was believed, lived by a different value system than did middle-class Northern shopkeepers. Aristocrats were more refined in their manners, more respectful of women, less dominated by materialistic factors, more skillful in such gentlemanly pursuits as fencing and riding, more inclined to defend their "honor," and—above all—more likely to be attracted to, and to be better fitted by nature for, a military career.

Ritchie Devon Watson, Jr., in his book *The Cavalier in Virginia Fiction*, has traced the development of the "myth of the Old Dominion." "The most potent and evocative projection of the mythical aristocrat," he writes, "has been the Virginia Cavalier," who became "the most magnetic symbol" of the aristocratic ideal. So strong was this myth that thirty years before the Civil War the figure of the Virginia cavalier as the embodiment of medieval knightly virtues was solidly embedded in the American mind. "By 1832," writes Watson, "there were precious few minds capable of being objective about Virginia, and in the following three decades objectivity in Virginia fiction vanished altogether." Such writers as William Alexander Caruthers and John Esten Cooke portrayed the mythical "Virginia gentleman magnified to heroic proportions." Their novels helped to promote "a highly distorted view of pre–Civil War Virginia and, indirectly, of all southern society." The Old South in general, and Virginia in particular, was Arthur's Camelot reincarnated in nineteenth-century America. The cavaliers were latter-day Knights of the Round Table.

In contrast to the Southern cavalier stood the "Yankee"—the symbol of the North in general but especially of the Northeast and even more especially of New England. The Yankee was depicted in American fiction as the churlish, greedy, grasping offspring of materialistic, low-class Saxons. Whereas the Virginia cavalier devoted his days to the pursuit of the manly virtues, the Yankee was more likely to be drawn to the ledger book or the factory—occupations that removed him from contact with nature, weakened him physically, and dulled his zest for the active life. Such financial and industrial careers as Northerners were likely to pursue thus combined with their genetic (or "racial") characteristics to weaken the soldierly virtues of courage and self-discipline. In the nineteenth century, then, the assumption was that industry weakened a nation's military strength and made its people unfit for warfare. (This assumption was a major reason why many Confederates were not dismayed by the economic statistics contrasting the relative wealth of North and South.)

An interesting variation on this theme was offered to the Southern public in the fall of 1861 by "SOUTHWESTERN," the Nashville correspondent of the *Charleston Mercury*. Writing from the Tennessee capital on 21 October, SOUTHWESTERN argued that the war would cut off immigration to the Northern states and that, therefore, the two sides would have to rely on their native population and its natural growth to provide the soldiers for a long war. Although the Northern states would be starting with a larger population base, S O U T H W E S T E R N maintained, the long-run odds were all in favor of the South. In such a fecundity contest, he believed, the Southerners would easily outperform their rivals because "people in towns and cities, in manufactures and commerce, don't increase like country people." Obviously he believed that the Rebels could do more than outfight the Yankees. To ensure victory, however, S O U T H - W E S T E R N recommended that every Confederate soldier be furloughed sometime during the next year for two to four weeks "in order that the married men should attend to their domestic affairs, and the unmarried—marry." By adopting such a plan, he concluded, the Rebels "would . . . come out of the war with a population undiminished, and carry it [the war] on indefinitely, with the same result."

Another widespread belief grew from the nineteenth-century assumption that Northern society was more "democratic"—by which people meant egalitarian and free—and the South was more "aristocratic"—meaning hierarchical. Democracy, many nineteenth-century Americans assumed, was corrosive of social discipline. It therefore followed that a democratic society would be less warlike and less amenable to military discipline than would an aristocratic society, in which every gentleman was a leader by birth and was expected to acquire martial skills as a part of his education. The common people in an aristocratic society were expected to obey those who were their betters. The common people in a democratic society were accustomed to acting pretty much as they pleased.

By the time of the Civil War many Northerners had also come to believe that the aristocratic Southern slaveholders had been plotting secession for decades and that they had been preparing for war during the antebellum years. Thus they had sent their sons off to West Point or to one of the state or private military schools that flourished across Dixie, they had equipped their states for war, they had organized and trained vast military forces, and they had honeycombed the Virginia countryside with impregnable fortifications. (Somehow it escaped notice that Virginia did not leave the Union until after the Civil War had begun.)

In summary, ninteenth-century Americans in both North and South accepted the idea that Southerners in general and Virginians in particular were especially suited to warfare by both biology and environment. Alongside this cavalier myth went the concomitant belief that Northerners in general and those from the Northeast in particular were peculiarly unfit for the military life.

Taken together, the contrasting ideas of cavalier and Yankee—which twentieth-century scholars have repeatedly demonstrated were almost without historical foundation—gave the Southerners hope in their struggle for independence and created some severe psychological problems for the Northerners. These ideas were especially inimical to the Federals in the East. Most of the Yankees who fought on the Virginia front came from the more industrialized areas of the North—Pennsylvania, New Jersey, New York, New England. If industrialization sapped a people's vigor and aptitude for the military, the areas with the greatest concentrations of industry must, therefore, produce the most languorous people—those least suited to be soldiers.

Fate, geography, economic development, and mythology thus all combined to pit "those Union soldiers with the least confidence . . . [against] the rebels with the most self-esteem—in Virginia." (Somehow, people on both sides managed to forget that the Old Dominion was by far the most industrialized part of the Confederacy.)

Events in Virginia early in the war seemed to substantiate these beliefs and to set the pattern for much of what followed. Early in the summer of 1861, as he prepared to send his army into the first major battle of the war, Irvin McDowell wrote, "The consequences of that battle will be of the greatest importance to the country, as establishing the prestige in this contest on the one side or the other." General Viscount Wolseley of the British army put the matter in a broader perspective when he observed, "Victories gained . . . early in a war engender that feeling of self-confidence which is, in fact, the twin brother of success." The reverse, of course, is true for lost battles.

The crushing Yankee defeats at First Manassas on 21 July 1861 and at Ball's Bluff three months later convinced many in the North that "the old fears of Southern military skill and preparations were justified." "The invincibility of landed society seemed apparent."

As other defeats on eastern battlefields followed, the Northerners developed great respect for the gallant "Southrons" in general and for the valiant Virginians in particular. Lee and Stonewall Jackson became heroic figures even among the Yankees. Jeb Stuart was of almost the same legendary stature. "Wherever Stuart rides," lamented a Northern minister in 1864, "he carries terror with him. His victories are half won before he strikes a blow. Our soldiers feel that he may pounce on them at any minute, and that he is as resistless as a hawk in a fowl yard."

Major General George B. McClellan was especially imbued with the belief in Southern martial superiority and with the equally debilitating idea that Northern democracy had so sapped the strength and fiber of the Federal soldiers that they were not the equals of their aristocratic opponents. Adams attributes a large part of McClellan's habitual overcaution to the general's belief that he faced an enemy army that was not only much larger than his own but one that also sprang from a militarily much more efficient people.

McClellan's enervating inferiority complex was transmitted to other officers—especially to the senior generals—of the Army of the Potomac, and it continued to exert a profound and depressing influence on them long after McClellan himself had left the army. As a result, the eastern Yankees came to think of themselves as inherently inferior to their opponents. The base, consumptive, huddled, miserable, demoralized wretches from the Northern cities therefore went into battle against Lee and his paladins in awe of their enemies and with the conviction that they were already whipped. "The one real advantage that Lee and his army had over their opponents," writes Adams, "was self-confidence."

This set of beliefs did not handicap the western Federals to as great an extent. Adams points out that the men of Michigan, Wisconsin, Indiana, Iowa, Illinois, and other western states were far less likely to be afflicted with self-doubt than were their eastern counterparts, whose society was experiencing the insidious effects of industrialization and urbanization. Western Unionists were also more likely to live closer to the soil and to practice (or at least to profess) the traditional rural virtues. They therefore had less cause to fear that their manly instincts had been weakened. Indeed, to the extent that they subscribed to the long-standing agrarian myth that nature had made American yeoman farmers into superior soldiers, they could think of them-selves as better fighters than their opponents, who came from a region where slavery had corrupted both their society and their moral strength. Finally, the Yankees in the West did not have to face the chivalrous Virginians on the battlefield, and they enjoyed early military successes in the Civil War. Their morale, therefore, was good from the start and got better as their armies advanced and victory followed upon victory.

Because the Southerners shared the same beliefs, the ideas that Adams describes tended to work in reverse for the Confed-erates. Rebels in the Old Dominion were much more likely to think of themselves as superior to their opponents; western Con-federates were far more prone to envision themselves as not quite the equivalents of the noble cavaliers of Virginia. The costly defeats suffered by the Rebels in the West in the early battles and the fact that few of their generals were from the Old Dominion reinforced their pessimism.

Ulysses S. Grant, who was born in Ohio and lived in the West for most of his life, was the first Federal general in the East "to remain immune to . . . the Virginia mentality," writes Adams. In 1864, when Grant came east to direct Union military operations in the Old Dominion, the Army of Northern Virginia "could no longer rely on the mental intimidation of its opponent to compensate for its own weakness in numerical strength."

Even the eventual Union victory, however, did not end the Federals' earlier way of thinking about the struggle between North and South. Many of the eastern Yankees did not like Grant, whom they saw as an uncouth westerner. Soon after the war they joined their former enemies in asserting that Grant had defeated Lee only by bludgeoning the gallant Virginian with superior numbers until he finally forced the Confederate leader to surrender. The widespread scandals of Grant's presidential administration (1869–77) helped to besmirch his reputation and to win for him the image of an unsavory character who was not fit company for any gentleman.

At about the same time, many Northern intellectuals, including such writers as Henry Adams and Henry James, were rapidly becoming disgusted at the materialism of late nineteenth-century America. They therefore came increasingly to look to the antebellum South and its people—especially the Virginia aristocrats—as "moral references by which the failures of American society [in their own day] might be better judged." Such Southern writers as the Virginians Thomas Nelson Page and Mary Johnston also helped to perpetuate the same idea.

Antebellum Virginia cavaliers thus came to be viewed as a noble band of men who clung to the eternal virtues and who were free of the crass, corrupting materialism that had so polluted postwar American society. Lee and his army, as the embodiments of this belief, marched out of history and into mythology. They came to represent not only a gallant military force of chivalrous, knightly gentlemen but also a noble, pure civilization that, after a heroic fight, had been crushed beneath the crude and repulsive juggernaut of nineteenth-century materialism and was gone with the wind.

No one ever regarded the western Rebels in the same light, and they were largely ignored by the makers of Southern mythology. In the most popular and famous of Civil War novels, it is the genteel, refined Ashley Wilkes who goes nobly to fight in Virginia even though he has serious doubts about the ultimate success of the Confederate cause. The rakish and, by genteel standards, ne'er-do-well Rhett Butler—who spent the early part of the war enriching himself through blockade running—winds up in the Army of Tennessee.[9]

PROBABLY the most important way in which Northerners helped to determine the different fates of the two major Confederate armies came from the active and fertile mind of Major General Henry Wager Halleck. A New Yorker and an 1839 graduate of the Military Academy, Halleck had enjoyed an enviable life before the Civil War. Most of his antebellum military career had been spent in engineering and staff assignments. He had resigned from the army in 1854, and for the next seven years he lived in California, where he had made a fortune in business. Meanwhile, his writings on military subjects and constitutional and mining law had won for him a great reputation as an intellectual.

In 1861, on the recommendation of Winfield Scott, then the commanding general of the army, President Lincoln appointed Halleck a major general. In November 1861, Halleck was placed in command of the Department of the Missouri—a post that gave him general authority over Federal military operations in West Tennessee and along the central portion of the Mississippi River as well as over those in Missouri.

Early in 1862 three of Halleck's subordinates—Samuel R. Curtis in Missouri, John Pope along the Mississippi, and Ulysses S. Grant in West Tennessee—won a string of important victories that secured Federal control of the area. Halleck, who handled the overall administration and organization rather than the details of the campaigns, received much of the credit for their successes. That spring Halleck took command of a field army and led a very cautious advance on the important rail center of

Corinth, Mississippi. After the Confederates evacuated Corinth, Halleck was called to Washington and given the position of general in chief of the Federal armies.

Halleck spent the remainder of the war in Washington, acting after early 1864 as chief of staff for Ulysses S. Grant, who by then had been promoted to lieutenant general and placed in charge of all Federal military activities. Halleck found his niche in Washington. As Stephen Ambrose, his biographer, has noted, he liked and thrived on Washington's seamy political intrigue.

Halleck's pompous manner and his physical appearance—stooped, flabby, balding, pop-eyed, rotund—along with his well-earned reputation as a paper-shuffling, pedantic, scheming, shifty, devious bureaucrat anxious above all else to avoid responsibility, led to his being held in low esteem by many of his Washington contemporaries. He impressed one reporter as "a cold, calculating owl." Lincoln came eventually to regard him as "little more than a first rate clerk." Secretary of War Edwin M. Stanton called him "probably the greatest scoundrel and most bare-faced villain in America." Navy Secretary Gideon Welles remarked that Halleck "originates nothing, anticipates nothing . . . takes no responsibility, plans nothing, suggests nothing, is good for nothing."

Historians, too, have usually disparaged Halleck. Bruce Catton called him "a flabby, moon-faced general . . . a solemn rumbling portentious pedant in uniform. . . . a born gossip and scold; nature had designed him to fill the part of a paper-pushing bureaucrat, and his mind was as orderly and tidy as its range was limited." T. Harry Williams observed that "Halleck had the reputation of being the most unpopular man in Washington. It was a title he worked hard to deserve. Surly and gruff in manner, he had no restraints about insulting people, even important government officials. He detested politicians and let them know it."

Despite his many shortcomings as a human being, Halleck made two important contributions to Union military success. He was a competent administrator. Ambrose calls him "the organizer, the coordinator, the planner, the manager." His constant insistence upon order and discipline instilled a much greater degree of administrative efficiency into the North's military effort than it otherwise would have exhibited. His work in reforming the system of promotions was especially noteworthy.

Halleck's other contribution was even more crucial than his administrative reforms and far more relevant to this study. He reached the conclusion—either by the time he arrived in Washington or soon afterward—that the route to Federal victory lay in the West. This idea, at least in its general scope, was not original with Halleck. Indeed, at the very beginning of the war, old Winfield Scott, still sharp in mind if lame in body, had proposed basically the same strategy in what came to be derided in the press as the "Anaconda plan." Scott wanted to establish a tight naval blockade all along the Confederate coast, organize a well-trained army, and then move down the Mississippi River with a strong column. Once the Federals had established their control over the Mississippi, Scott believed, the Confederacy—isolated from the world and cut in twain—would abandon its quest for independence as Southern Unionists overthrew the secessionists and reestablished loyal governments in the seceded states. Scott planned to hold Washington securely, but he did not envision any major offensive action in Virginia.

The origins of Halleck's belief about the West are unknown. It is possible that he saw the war in the same way that Scott had seen it or that his 1861–62 experiences in the Mississippi Valley led him to view the West as the area in which the North had its greatest opportunity. Halleck may have concluded that military operations in the West offered greater hope of success because the meddling politicians in Washington would be less likely to interfere with armies operating at great distances from the capital.

It is also possible that Halleck, too, believed that the inferior Northerners from the eastern Federal states could not defeat the chivalrous Rebels in Virginia or that he simply observed the military equilibrium that had been reached on the eastern front, where, by the summer of 1862, two major Union drives against

Richmond had been defeated and a third was about to be. Halleck could have based his thinking on the writings of the military theorist Baron Antoine Henri Jomini (some of whose works Halleck had translated into English), who advised, among other strategies, concentration of strength against the weakest points of the enemy. Since the Rebels had already demonstrated their strength in Virginia, the Federals might do well to shift their emphasis to some other area.

Halleck also observed that the West offered strategic opportunities that did not exist in Virginia. The capture of Richmond, for example, might not accomplish much in a purely military sense because the Confederates could easily transfer their base of operations to some other nearby point on the Old Dominion's rail network and continue the war pretty much as before. For the Federals to assemble a force strong enough to take the Rebel capital would necessitate their stripping troops from the defenses of Washington, and the Southerners might then capture that city. This "swapping of queens," Halleck concluded, would not accomplish much. The capture of key western cities, however, would cut the Rebel railroads and make it impossible for the Confederates to keep their armies supplied across the vast distance between the Appalachians and the Mississippi. The Rebel armies would, therefore, disintegrate as the task of keeping them fed and clothed became increasingly difficult.

Whatever the origin of his conviction, Halleck's arrival in Washington marked the beginning of a transformation of Federal strategy and a consequent shifting of emphasis and resources to support military operations in the West. By the end of 1862 Lincoln, who, indeed, may already have had inclinations in favor of the West, was well along toward adopting a strategy that involved acceptance of a stalemate in Virginia and a concentration of effort and resources in the West.

Implementation of this "Lincoln-Halleck" policy meant that for the last two and a half years of the war the Yankees were making their major effort against the western Rebels. Even Grant's bloody 1864–65 campaign in Virginia was waged more to keep Lee from sending away troops to reinforce other areas and to pacify Northern public opinion, which expected and demanded a large-scale, highly visible military effort against the enemy capital, than with the expectation that it would produce results—as, indeed, it did not. By the end of 1864, with his army bogged down in the trenches at Petersburg, Grant himself came to share that outlook. "Grant stood still," notes his most recent biographer, "so that others . . . could move." "The unhappy Army of the Potomac," wrote Bruce Catton, "which was to do the worst of the fighting and suffer the heaviest casualties, was not, in the end, actually required to do anything more than hold the line in front of Washington."[10]

Adoption of the western strategy by the Federal government also meant that the Confederacy—already by far the weaker of the two warring powers—faced its enemy's main strength at its own weakest point. There is no evidence that the Southerners ever realized what was happening, although Rebel Secretaries of War George W. Randolph and James A. Seddon waged a heroic bureaucratic battle in an effort to get the Confederate government to devote more attention to matters in the West. Certainly the Rebel authorities never made a corresponding decision to concentrate the greater part of their military strength in the West, even though such a policy was strenuously advocated throughout the war by a "western concentration bloc" of Confederate generals and politicians. Indeed, the reverse was often the case because several of the decisions made by the Confederate government had the unintended side effect of weakening Rebel power in the West, where the Confederates were already facing more problems than they were capable of handling.

CHAPTER FOUR

Confederate Contributions

From the beginning of the Civil War to its end, one side effect of several of the decisions, practices, and policies of the Confederate government was the hampering of the Army of Tennessee. Such a consequence, of course, was not intended by any of the Rebel officials who set the policies and made the decisions, and many of the problems that arose from the government's actions were not unique to the western army. The Army of Northern Virginia, however, was the beneficiary of some of these government policies, and it was less hurt by many others than was the Army of Tennessee.

The earliest—and for the western Rebels probably the most damaging—government decision concerned the location of the Southerners' national capital. The first Confederate capital was Montgomery, Alabama. The city had been chosen as the place to organize the new government because it was conveniently lo-cated near the geographical center of the first six states that seceded. Once the Confederate government was organized, it remained in Montgomery for only about three months.

Shortly after Virginia left the Union, Rebel political authorities decided to transfer their seat of government to Richmond. There were several compelling arguments behind their action. Mont-gomery, with a total population of only about nine thousand, was too small to house a national government with its soon-to-be-bloated bureaucracy, its politicians, its lobbyists, its profiteers, and its assorted other hangers-on. Alabama's capital city was uncomfortable—hot, humid, crowded, dirty, and insect-plagued. Once secession had run its course, moreover, Montgomery was judged to be too far removed from any of the likely areas of major military operations.

Richmond, by contrast, was much larger (thirty-eight thousand people in 1860), and, with its long history and its stately public buildings, it was far more imposing. Its society was much more sophisticated and cosmopolitan. It was located very close to the area that was widely expected to be the main scene of military action, and it was—with the possible exception of New Orleans—the most important economic and industrial city in the Confederacy. Rebel authorities, furthermore, had virtually promised the capital to Virginia to secure the Old Dominion's secession. Transfer of the seat of government northward would also put the Confederate government in much closer contact with possible sources of help in Europe, demonstrate to the Virginia public that the Southerners were serious about defending the Old Dominion, and help to eradicate the widespread impression that secession was nothing more than the temper tantrum of a few hotheaded demagogues from the Cotton South.

Several historians of the war have questioned the wisdom of the decision to move the capital—or at least the wisdom of locating it in Richmond. They have pointed to the danger inherent in the situation when a new, relatively weak nation locates its seat of government in a city so close to its frontier with a much stronger hostile power. Establishment of the government in Richmond, they argue, isolated the Confederate authorities from the vital areas in the West and gave them a myopic outlook that led to an overemphasis on the war in Virginia and a consequent neglect of the West. Located in Richmond, the capital drew the Northern armies, and its symbolic importance became so great that it had to be defended long after purely military factors dictated some other course of action.

It seems more likely, however, that removal of the capital to Richmond played only a minor role in making the city a major military objective of the Yankee armies. Richmond's proximity to the Confederate frontier, her great industrial importance, and her place in the Southern railroad network would have both necessitated that she be defended at all costs and drawn Northern public opinion and military forces against her even if the

Rebels had located their national capital in Wetumpka, Alabama.

Relocation of the capital to Virginia did, however, have one minor and one significant military effect. To the extent that it attracted Yankee efforts and resources to the Old Dominion, it served to draw Federal forces into the theater of war where the Rebels were best situated to deal with them, and in that way, it worked to the Southerners' advantage. Having the capital in Richmond, however, also guaranteed that the Rebel army in Virginia would be the object of much greater official and public attention than would Confederate military forces operating outside the Old Dominion. The nearest danger is often the one most clearly perceived, and the most clearly perceived danger is usually the one that receives the most attention. Even after the Federal government decided to concentrate its efforts in the West, Confederate officials and Rebel public opinion usually continued to focus a disproportionate share of their attention on the Old Dominion. The frequent, exhilarating military successes that the Southerners won in Virginia in 1861, 1862, and early 1863 reinforced this pattern.[1]

THE way the Confederate government organized its land military forces militated against successful operations in the West. The basic problem was that for much of the war there was no effective organization of Confederate forces outside Virginia above the level of individual field armies. President Jefferson Davis adopted a system to divide the Confederacy into territorial commands called departments. A prominent, high-ranking general officer was placed in charge of each department and of the troops assigned to it, and his department's boundaries were clearly defined and announced to the country. Most of the troops in a given department operated as a field army to defend the area; others were used as garrisons for important points or in various administrative tasks. Each department, its commander, and its army, were usually independent of the surrounding departments. It was the president's hope that each department would furnish food for its own troops. Davis regarded himself as literally the commander in chief of the Confederate military forces, and for most of the war he sought to coordinate army movements across departmental lines from his office in Richmond.

This policy was based on several assumptions. First, the president believed, the Northerners could make but one major effort at a time. They would, therefore, have to strip troops from other areas to concentrate their forces at the point they had selected for the attack. Second, Davis assumed, the Southerners would be able to ascertain where the enemy intended to strike. Once the point of the enemy's attack was known, the Rebel government would advise commanders in unthreatened areas, and, Davis thought, they would rush reinforcements to their colleague whose department was menaced by the enemy. After the Federal offensive had been defeated, the reinforcements would return to their own department, where they would wait while the Federals regrouped for another effort, and then the whole process would begin again. Eventually, the Yankees would realize that they could not conquer the South, and they would give up and allow the Southern Confederacy to go its separate way. The system could also be used to concentrate troops for an offensive movement with units from two or more departments combining temporarily for a quick strike at the enemy.

In theory such an arrangement should have worked adequately; in practice, it quickly became clear, it contained several serious flaws. The basic problem with Davis's scheme was that the Northerners were so superior in numbers and matériel that they were able to mount simultaneous threats against more than one point. In the winter of 1863–64, for example, while the Confederates debated whether the Yankees' major effort would be made in Virginia or Georgia, the Federals were busy organizing massive offensive movements in both areas. They also planned to distract the Rebels with lesser campaigns at several other points around the Confederacy's periphery so that the Southerners would be prevented from transferring reinforcements from one point to another.

Even had Davis's first assumption been correct, his entire

strategic system would have been dependent on the collection at Richmond of accurate information about the enemy's intentions and the correct evaluation and interpretation of that information by the president and the War Department. Collection of information from areas distant from the capital was often impeded by inadequate communications and by the reluctance of some of the generals to communicate fully and freely with the government. In some cases the generals in the field did not realize what was happening in their front, and, even had they desired to do so, they could not have provided Davis with accurate intelligence upon which to base his decisions (see Chapter 8).

As a result, the information available to Davis and his advisers was often distorted. The closeness of the Virginia front to the capital and the consequent deluge of information from that area as well as the greater cooperation between the Virginia army and the government and the greater personal compatibility between the president and General Robert E. Lee all meant that Davis was far better informed about what was transpiring in Virginia than he was about events in Tennessee, Mississippi, or Georgia. Under the circumstances, the president naturally came to focus more on developments on the eastern front, and his understanding of what was happening elsewhere was often very limited.

Other problems also plagued the system. Even if Davis managed correctly to decipher Federal intentions, there was no assurance that other Rebels would concur in his interpretation of the enemy's schemes or that they would wholeheartedly work to carry out the president's plan to meet the enemy threat. Davis sometimes made the situation even worse because he often worded instructions in such a way that the department commanders seemed to have discretion about whether to obey them. A message from the president to send "any available" reinforcements—or to send help "if practicable"—to the commander of another department was subject to the interpretation that no reinforcements were available or that it was not practicable to send away any troops.

Confederate Contributions

What followed would not have surprised anyone who has ever worked in a military headquarters and dealt with subordinate commanders. Almost every officer believes that his command is the most important one and that it is menaced by virtually the entire military force of the enemy. He is, therefore, very reluctant to part with any of his troops for even a short while. Not surprisingly, a request from Davis to send troops from one department to reinforce another was sometimes ignored by the commander from whom the troops were to come and, in many other cases, was followed by a telegraphic debate between that commander and the president over whether to send the troops. It often took the Richmond authorities many messages and several days to pry loose the troops who were supposed to be rushed from one department to help defend another.

Even when reinforcements were finally made ready, Davis's system often foundered when the rickety Rebel railroads proved unable to transport the troops across the great distances of the western Confederacy in time to do much good. Many historians have pointed to the "interior lines of communication" as a great Southern advantage that could be used to offset Northern numerical superiority by making it possible quickly to shift Confederate troops from one important point to another. In fact, such an advantage existed mostly in Virginia, where the narrow eastern theater of operations and the Old Dominion's rail network made such movements of troops practicable. In the vast reaches of the West, the Confederates were often compelled to use very inefficient exterior lines of communication and transportation. After early 1862, when the Yankees controlled many of the important western rivers, there were no interior lines in the West for the Confederates to use. As Allan Nevins pointed out, the South's interior lines in the West "lost meaning when a Union army moved up the Tennessee into the heart of the Confederacy." If one measures the Rebels' western lines of communication by the true standard—time, not distance—it is clear that the Southerners assigned to defend the area between the Alleghenies and the

Mississippi were operating at a great disadvantage. As the war went on and the condition of the railroads deteriorated, the system became even less workable.

Three examples will illustrate some of the difficulties inherent in Davis's system. In the summer and fall of 1862 the Confederates organized a massive offensive in the West that was designed to force the Yankees out of Tennessee and Kentucky. Brigadier General Humphrey Marshall was to lead a column from western Virginia into Kentucky. Major General Edmund Kirby Smith was to march from his East Tennessee Department into the Bluegrass. General Braxton Bragg was to bring the Army of Tennessee all the way from Mississippi to cooperate with Marshall and Smith in Kentucky. Meanwhile, in North Mississippi, Major Generals Earl Van Dorn and Sterling Price were to move against the Federals there to keep them from sending help to their comrades who were being assailed by Marshall, Smith, and Bragg. Davis believed that he could rely on his generals to cooperate voluntarily, and he did not appoint anyone to command the operation. Not surprisingly, the Confederate offensive quickly degenerated into spastic, uncoordinated efforts. Although the Rebels managed to win some battles, their victories were unexploited by their generals. Other battles were lost. Several thousand good troops died to no purpose, and the whole enterprise was a miserable failure.

A second example took place in December 1862, when the Rebel government ordered that Major General Carter L. Stevenson's division be sent from the Army of Tennessee, then posted near Murfreesboro, Tennessee, to western Mississippi, where, it was believed, the Federals were massing for an attack. The generals of the Army of Tennessee protested and urged that the reinforcements be taken from some other command. President Davis overruled them. On 18 December the division began its three-week rail journey from central Tennessee to Jackson, Mississippi, traveling via Chattanooga, Atlanta, Montgomery, Mobile, and Meridian—hardly an interior line. While Stevenson's men were en route, the Yankees in Mississippi were repulsed at Chickasaw Bluffs, and the Confederates in Tennessee were defeated in a battle at Murfreesboro. The division had left too soon to be of help in Tennessee and arrived too late to be of assistance in Mississippi. It was kept in Mississippi, and a few months later it was captured at Vicksburg.

A similar instance arose early in 1864, when the Northerners advanced eastward from the Mississippi River, threatening the Confederates in eastern Mississippi and western Alabama. The government ordered General Joseph E. Johnston, commanding the Army of Tennessee at Dalton, Georgia, to send reinforcements to Alabama. Johnston, however, believed his position at Dalton to be threatened, and he hesitated to send away any of his troops. Several days of debate over the telegraph lines followed before Davis finally gave Johnston a peremptory order to send three divisions to Alabama. Soon after the troops had left, the Yankees at Chattanooga launched a reconnaissance in force against Johnston, who quickly fired off desperate telegrams to recall his absent divisions. By the time they got back to Dalton, both Federal raids had ended.

There were two other problems with Davis's departmental system. Responsibility for Confederate defense was sometimes divided in such a way that successful resistance to any determined enemy advance was most unlikely. In 1863, for example, the defense of the east and west banks of the Mississippi River was entrusted to the commanders of two separate departments. For the commander on the eastern side, defense of the river and of the key city of Vicksburg was a major goal. The commander on the western side, however, was preoccupied with events elsewhere. The result was that the Southerners never developed any coordinated defense, and the great river fell into Federal control when the Yankees under Grant "split the seam" between the two Rebel departments by advancing down the western bank of the river to gain positions from which they could cross to conquer the eastern side.

A final problem with the system was its rigidity in a war that was often characterized by a very fluid military situation—especially in the West. A Confederate army might be forced to retreat quickly from its department or be driven to a position that left it isolated from a part of the area it was supposed to protect. In such a situation Rebel authorities needed to react quickly to realign departmental boundaries and reallocate responsibility for defense and logistics lest a vacuum be created that was beyond the authority of any commander. For example, in late 1863 the Army of Tennessee was driven back into North Georgia. At that time the Department of Tennessee included a strip of counties along the south bank of the Tennessee River in North Alabama. Once the Army of Tennessee was posted in North Georgia, it was almost completely cut off from the North Alabama counties that it was supposed to protect. This situation lasted for several months until Rebel authorities in Richmond got around to redrawing departmental boundaries. Meanwhile, no Confederate commander exercised effective control along the south side of the Tennessee River. Without adequate reconnaissance in the area, the Southerners did not fathom the developing Federal plans for the opening of the 1864 campaign. As a result, the Army of Tennessee was caught woefully off guard in May 1864 and forced to abandon its strongly fortified positions around Dalton, Georgia.

The western Rebels' basic problem was divided responsibility. The Confederate departmental system in Virginia had begun with a plethora of small departments, but Davis soon began to combine them. In late 1861 and early 1862 he swept the hitherto independent Departments of Fredericksburg, Alexandria, the Peninsula, and Norfolk, along with the Valley District, into the newly created Department of Northern Virginia. The president also combined several smaller commands to form the Department of North Carolina and Southern Virginia; the Department of South Carolina, Georgia, and Florida; and the Department of the Trans-Mississippi.

Davis never created a large number of very small departments between the Appalachians and the Mississippi, but he was never willing to organize any real overall command structure for the area either. Perhaps the president believed that the West was too vast for a single commander to exercise all the administrative, logistical, and command functions for which the general of a field army was responsible. For most of the war there were three independent Rebel commands in the region. East Tennessee was usually separate. The Confederate forces operating in Alabama, Mississippi, and East Louisiana constituted a separate command. After the first year of the war, the Department of Tennessee occupied the middle portion of the West.

On three occasions Davis sought to provide better control for the West by placing a general over several of the western departments and giving him vague supervisory authority to coordinate their operations. In the fall of 1861 the president assigned General Albert Sidney Johnston to command all of the Confederate forces between the Appalachian Mountains on the east and the Ozarks on the west. From late 1862 until mid-1863 General Joseph E. Johnston was supposed to coordinate Rebel military activities in Tennessee, Alabama, and Mississippi. The same areas, along with parts of Georgia, were included in the Military Division of the West, which Davis created in October 1864 and placed under the command of General Pierre G. T. Beauregard.

None of these experiments in a unified western command worked. In some cases responsibility for the failures lay with the Richmond authorities; at other times the generals were clearly at fault; more often, both the president and the War Department on one hand and the generals on the other were to blame. Orders establishing the western commands were sometimes unclear in delineating the extent of the commander's authority over the separate forces operating in the West. In the summer of 1863, for example, the government gave the commander of the Army of Tennessee authority over the Department of East Tennessee, but it did not specify whether the East Tennessee command had been abolished.

On several occasions the government did not clearly specify priorities for the western commanders to follow. In 1863 Joseph E. Johnston, realizing that he could not hold both, asked point-blank whether he should give up Tennessee or the Mississippi River. President Davis replied with the meaningless message that "to hold the Mississippi is vital."

Much of this confusion grew from the authorities' ignorance about the West in general and the Army of Tennessee in particular. Often the Richmond officials were unable to comprehend the difficulties faced by the Rebels in the West. They seemed unable to grasp the fact that the western railroads could not move troops quickly over the long, roundabout route from central Tennessee to central Mississsippi and that many of the lines on a map of Tennessee or Kentucky were the representations of crude dirt roads traversing rugged, barren mountains. If the Army of Tennessee could move at all on such roads, it would require good weather and several thousand wagons along with a corresponding number of horses or mules to transport its supplies, its pontoon bridges, its ammunition, and its medicines.

To make matters even worse, the Richmond authorities often ignored their own command structure and continued to receive reports directly from and to issue orders directly to subordinate generals in the West without bothering to inform the overall commander in the area. As a result, the western commander who was planning to use a particular unit for some purpose might discover that the president had ordered the same unit off on another mission. In the spring of 1863, for example, the Confederates operating in Mississippi sent reports of events in their front to Richmond but not to Joseph E. Johnston, who—in theory at least—exercised command over them.

Late in 1861 Albert Sidney Johnston posted himself at Bowling Green, Kentucky, where he became isolated from the rest of his command and almost totally absorbed with the threat to that Rebel outpost. As a result, there was no one exercising effective command in the West during the crucial winter of 1861–62. A year later Joseph E. Johnston questioned the arrangement of his command. He favored a union of the Trans-Mississippi troops with those assigned to defend the east bank of the great river rather than Davis's arrangement to provide cooperation between the armies in Tennessee and Mississippi. Johnston devoted much of his time to complaining about what he regarded as the unworkableness of the command scheme for the West. He could get no clear statement from the government as to what he was expected to do, and for personal reasons he did not get along well with the president. He was, therefore, unwilling to do very much without explicit authority lest he be criticized by the chief executive. Under both of the Johnstons the western Rebels suffered disasters. Beauregard was also given only a vague mandate to supervise the West. He, too, neither liked nor trusted the president, who reciprocated the feeling. By the time his command was created in late 1864, the Rebel military position in the West had deteriorated so much that it is doubtful if anything could have helped.

Of course, Davis's system did not always result in failure. Its greatest success came in September 1863, when troops were transferred from Virginia and other areas to Georgia to help the Army of Tennessee win its great victory at Chickamauga. Even so, a long debate among Confederate leaders over whether troops should be sent from Virginia almost delayed their departure until it would have been too late for them to arrive in time. As it was, only a part of the reinforcements from Virginia (five of ten brigades of infantry but none of the artillery) reached the Army of Tennessee in time to be of help in the battle.

Davis's scheme did work on several other occasions, when troops were moved in time to be effective. The system of shuffling men about to threatened points, however, was far more likely to work in Virginia and the eastern Confederacy than it was in the West. Compared to the West, the area of military operations in Virginia was very small, and almost all of it was in the Department of Northern Virginia and hence clearly under the authority of one general.

Even when separate commands were maintained in the area where the Army of Northern Virginia was operating, such as the Department of Henrico, they were so obviously insignificant and so closely connected with the overall defense of Richmond that they were usually made subordinate to the main Confederate commander in the region. Therefore, a Federal force operating against the eastern Confederacy in Virginia was in a relatively confined area opposed by Confederate troops who were usually under the control of one commander.

The presence of the Rebel government in nearby Richmond and the politicians' natural desire to protect the capital also ensured that cooperation between the Southern forces in Virginia and the troops in the Department of North Carolina and Southern Virginia—and sometimes even troops from the Department of South Carolina, Georgia, and Florida—was much better than was usually the case in other areas of the Confederacy. In the spring of 1864, for example, units rushed northward from the Carolinas played a key role in saving Petersburg and Richmond from the Yankees.

The western Rebels did not benefit from either unity of command or a nearby government to coordinate their activities. In the spring of 1864, even as troops from the Carolinas were hastening to the defense of the capital, the Army of Tennessee was attempting to protect Atlanta and North Georgia. An obvious strategy for the Rebels to use was to send the cavalry force from the Department of Alabama, Mississippi, and East Louisiana to operate against the railroads that snaked back across North Georgia, Alabama, Tennessee, and Kentucky to supply the invading Yankees in North Georgia. Because these cavalrymen were in an independent department, however, the commander of the Army of Tennessee could not order them sent against his opponent's rail line. He could only suggest, request, plead, and beg that they be so employed. The commander of the Department of Alabama, Mississippi, and East Louisiana expressed his sympathies and promised to do what he could. He was kept busy, however, repelling Yankee raids into his own area—raids that were designed to keep his cavalry occupied in Mississippi and, therefore, off the Federal railroads in Tennessee and Kentucky. As a result, the Army of Tennessee never got the help its commander requested.

The Army of Northern Virginia operated in a small geographical area under a de facto unified command system that usually gave its commander control over all of the area that was vital to his operations and of the troops in it. The western Rebels enjoyed no such good fortune. Confederate policies often worked to keep them divided and in pursuit of different objectives. Their situation was made even more unfavorable by the gradual evolution of a unified command structure by the Federals so that after late 1863 all Northern forces between the Appalachians and the Mississippi were controlled by one man. The same Yankee general who directed the campaign against Atlanta also ordered the raids that tied down the Rebel cavalry in Mississippi. His Confederate counterpart could only watch, helpless to take appropriate countermeasures.[2]

CONFEDERATE logistical policies also hampered the Army of Tennessee throughout the war. At the beginning of the conflict the government adopted the policy of having the Army of Tennessee draw its food supply from the northern part of Tennessee, near which it was then deployed. Food collected from other parts of the western Confederacy was to be used to feed other troops. If crops were bad in the Army of Tennessee's area—as they were in 1861 and 1862, when a severe drought plagued the region—the western army might well go hungry. In the fall of 1862, while the Army of Tennessee was campaigning in Kentucky, supply agents sent out by the Richmond government went through Middle Tennessee. They were willing to pay higher prices than were the agents from the Army of Tennessee (Confederate supply operatives often found themselves in competition with each other). The Richmond agents were, therefore, able to purchase large quantities of wheat, flour, bacon, beef, and pork, which they shipped off to the supply depot in Atlanta to be held there pending requisition from other areas.

Meridian and Jackson, Mississippi, which had been supply depots for the Army of Tennessee in the summer of 1862 when it began its movement into Kentucky, were detached from that army's area of responsibility in the following October and included in a new command embracing Mississippi and East Louisiana. Chattanooga, which had become a temporary supply depot for the Army of Tennessee while it was campaigning in Kentucky, was under the jurisdiction of the Department of East Tennessee until it was added to the Department of Tennessee in early 1863. As a result, for a few months, the Army of Tennessee, in the words of its most recent historian, "no longer had a base."

In the summer of 1863 the western army was required to draw its supplies from an area that included East Tennessee, Georgia north and west of Atlanta, and North Alabama. Almost all of the Alabama part of the command and a good part of East Tennessee were soon overrun by the Yankees. The rest of Alabama, which had previously supplied some food to the Army of Tennessee, was then in another command. These changes meant that the Army of Tennessee was supposed to draw its supplies from a very limited area—considerably more limited than the region that supplied the much smaller army operating in the Department of Alabama, Mississippi, and East Louisiana. To make its situation even more frustrating, the Army of Tennessee found itself responsbile for protecting areas that provided supplies for other armies. Georgia, for example, which was defended on the northwest by the Army of Tennessee, provided supplies that went mostly to Virginia or to troops stationed along the South Atlantic Coast.

All armies have to defend their sources of supply, and sometimes their operations are shaped by the need to do so. Far more than most military forces, however, the Army of Tennessee found its government's supply system shaping its campaigns. In the first winter of the war the western army was forced into a rigid territorial defense to protect the southern Kentucky–northern Tennessee area whence came its foodstuffs. In early 1863 the Army of Tennessee was compelled to take up a position in the south central portion of its namesake state rather than in the foothills of the Cumberland Mountains because the former area was more likely to yield provisions. While in this area, the army had to disperse along a seventy-mile front to feed itself although from a military point of view it would have been far better to concentrate the army for its defense. The Army of Tennessee then wore out its horses and mules gathering food from this area and distributing it along its far-flung line. At that time the Rebel depot in Atlanta was shipping half a million pounds of meat to Virginia every week. Much of the meat sent from Atlanta was from the animals that the supply agents from Richmond had removed from Tennessee the previous fall.

Even in its death throes the Richmond government could not bring itself to give logistical equality to the Army of Tennessee. By early 1865 the effective area of the Confederate States of America had been reduced to a few thousand square miles of central North Carolina and southern Virginia and the two armies that were struggling there to hold back an avalanche of invading Yankees. General Joseph E. Johnston was assigned on 22 February to command the Rebel troops who were defending North Carolina. Johnston's small force included many of the remnants of the Army of Tennessee.

Upon assuming command, Johnston found that Confederate supply officers in North Carolina were under orders "to permit none of the provisions they collected in that State to be used by the troops serving in it." The commissary warehouses at Charlotte and Weldon, North Carolina, and Danville, Virginia, bulged with rations sufficient to feed 120,000 men for two months. All of these provisions, Johnston learned, were being held for the exclusive use of the Army of Northern Virginia.

This policy could, perhaps, be justified on the grounds that the troops in Virginia had to be fed from somewhere. The government's policy regarding the hoards of coffee, tea, sugar, and medicinal brandy that were stored in Charlotte, however, was completely inexplicable. These supplies belonged to the no longer existing Confederate navy. When Johnston asked that they be turned over to his army, his request was disapproved. Eventually these supplies were scattered by local civilians and by wandering soldiers. To add a final insult for the western Rebels, many of these wandering soldiers were men from the recently surrendered Virginia army, who were on their way from Appomattox to their homes in the Deep South.

Instead of supplying food for Johnston's troops, the government instructed that general to send out foraging parties from his own ranks to collect food for his men. The sparsely populated area, the activities of the Yankees, and the need to leave something for the Confederate civilians to eat all militated against supplying Johnston's army adequately and reduced the maneuverability of his columns. Johnston's men were fed only through the heroic work of some of the army's officers, the cooperation and diligent efforts of North Carolina state officials, and the bureaucratically brave decisions of some local supply officers, who ignored irrelevant instructions from the government and turned over to Johnston as much as possible of the supplies in their charge.

There was also something wrong with the Army of Tennessee's own system of supply. On 31 December 1862, almost two years after the Confederacy was organized, the Forty-fourth Mississippi Regiment was sent into the thick of the battle at Murfreesboro, Tennessee. The men of the regiment had been waiting for forty-eight hours in a shallow trench and had not been permitted to build fires. When the order came to advance, they rose up and charged across a cotton field against a very strong Federal artillery position and its infantry supports. The Mississippians charged armed only with sticks—they had no firearms.

Although no Confederate army ever lost a battle because it lacked adequate supplies, the Army of Tennessee—to a far greater degree than its counterpart in Virginia—found its freedom of maneuver circumscribed by its government's logistical policies. It is clear that when it came time to divide up the Confederacy's limited resources, the Army of Tennessee did not get its fair share.[3]

Confederate Contributions

CONFEDERATE government policies combined with Yankee decisions and geographical-political-economic-psychological factors to hamper the western Confederates in general and the Army of Tennessee in particular. Many of these same policies also benefited the Army of Northern Virginia.

None of these factors, however—or even all of them taken together—explain fully the differences between the two major Confederate armies. There was a much more simple and basic reason for the success enjoyed by the Confederates in the East: the Army of Northern Virginia was a better army than was the Army of Tennessee. "Grant has had his eyes opened," wrote George G. Meade to his wife on 5 June 1864, after a month of some of the bloodiest fighting in American history. "[He] is willing to admit that Virginia and Lee's army is not Tennessee and Bragg's army."[4]

The reasons for the superior quality of the Virginia army over its western counterpart are to be found in the history and personnel of the two great Rebel armies.

CHAPTER FIVE

History's Role

A rmies, like all human institutions, are to a great degree the products of their past. Although only a short time elapsed between the creation of the Confederacy and the organization of the Army of Northern Virginia and the Army of Tennessee, both of the Confederates' two major armies were built on preexisting historical foundations. The Army of Tennessee was to suffer greatly because it was built on a foundation of sand; the Army of Northern Virginia rested, by comparison, on a rock.

Each of the two major Confederate armies was built around the nucleus of a state military organization. There was an American tradition dating from the early colonial period and continuing on into the eighteenth and nineteenth centuries that each colony and then each state would provide a military force for its own defense against both outside invasion and local insurrections. In times of peace, these military forces remained under the control of the individual states. In times of war, the federal government would draw individuals and, sometimes, whole units from these state forces and organize them as a large national army.

There were two components of the prewar state military forces. By law, all able-bodied, free, white, adult males between eighteen and forty-five years of age were required to belong to the militia in the state where they lived. Members of the militias were supposed to assemble every so often for training, and the states were expected to see to it that adequate supplies of weapons, ammunition, and other equipment were available for use in any emergency. In practice, the militia was well organized, adequately equipped, and at least partially trained in some states and virtually nonexistent in others.

In many cases a state's military force also included a number of legislatively chartered but privately organized and maintained "volunteer" military companies. These elitist organizations often traced their lineage to the colonial or revolutionary periods, and membership in their ranks was by invitation only. The Chatham Artillery of Savannah, Georgia, for example, dated from 1778, and a person wishing to join its ranks had to have the sponsorship of two of the old members and a favorable vote by four-fifths of the unit before he would be accepted.

These volunteer units were frequently as much social and fraternal organizations as they were military companies. Their members enjoyed wearing their especially designed uniforms and valued the camaraderie that stemmed from participation in the unit's activities. Members of such units were exempt from normal militia duty. The volunteer companies often owned their own drill halls and armories, and they were allowed the use of public land as their parade grounds. Their drills were festive occasions, often followed by banquets, picnics, formal orations, concerts, soirées, or cotillions.

Frequently these well-drilled organizations were called upon to stage parades or fire salutes on such occasions as the funeral of some dignitary, the arrival in the city of a distinguished guest, the Fourth of July, George Washington's birthday, or the anniversary of Andrew Jackson's 8 January 1815 victory over the British in the Battle of New Orleans. Since these were volunteer units, their enthusiasm for the military life was great, and their esprit de corps was high. Such units were especially popular in the older, coastal regions of the South.[1]

As each of the Southern states seceded, it began to call its military forces to active duty. Three categories of military units responded to each state's call. Some militia units went bodily into the state service (although most of them served for only a short time); volunteer units rushed to the field; and each state began to raise new units—also called volunteers—made up of individuals (who would themselves be militiamen) especially recruited for the emergency. Most of the troops who served the South during the war were in this third type of unit. Many of the units in this third category were raised, organized, and sometimes equipped by private individuals, who then offered their services to the state. Although this process of raising a state military force went further in Tennessee and Virginia than it did in such isolated places as Texas and Florida, the result was the formation of a separate army for each seceded state.

Eventually almost all of the troops from each state's army were transferred to Confederate service. Until the transfer, however, each state force was independent and under the authority of its own commander—usually a state major general—who, in turn, was responsible to the governor, the state legislature, the state secession convention, an especially created "military board" or some other such authority. Because of this process, much of the tone, the attitude, and the early history of what became the Confederate Army of Tennessee was derived from the history of the "provisional army" organized in the late spring and summer of 1861 by the state of Tennessee and from that state's political and military leaders. Much of the tone, the attitude, and the early history of the Army of Northern Virginia was inherited from the political and military leaders of the Old Dominion and from the state army that they raised early in the war. The different backgrounds from which the two major Confederate armies came were to have profound effects both on their histories during the Civil War and on the war itself.

Both the Volunteer State and the Old Dominion were late in leaving the Union. Not until after the Confederate attack on Fort Sumter and President Lincoln's 15 April 1861 call for troops to be used against the already seceded states of the Deep South did Virginia and Tennessee act. On 17 April the Virginia State Convention voted to secede. On 6 May the Tennessee legislature adopted a "Declaration of Independence," declaring the Volunteer State to be out of the Union. Although both of these actions had to be ratified by the voters (on 23 May for Virginia; on 8 June for Tennessee), the action of the Virginia convention and the

Tennessee legislature marked the de facto secession of the two states.

EVEN before she left the Union, Virginia, with certainly the strongest military tradition of any Southern state, had a fairly well-developed militia. Indeed, in the 1859–61 period, in the wake of the abolitionist John Brown's attack on Harpers Ferry, the Old Dominion had experienced something of a renascence of its military strength. In the winter of 1859–60 both the outgoing governor, Henry A. Wise, and the incoming chief executive, John Letcher, called for a strengthening of and an improvement in the commonwealth's ability to defend itself. The state legislature, under the leadership of James L. Kemper, chairman of the Committee on Military Affairs of the House of Delegates, launched a program designed to reorganize and rebuild the Virginia militia. In early 1860 the legislature voted $500,000 for the purchase and manufacture of arms and an additional $20,000 to expand the Virginia Military Institute. A year later—still three months before the state seceded—the Old Dominion's lawmakers appropriated $800,000 to buy even more arms and $200,000 for coastal and river defense. On 20 April 1861, just after secession, the state legislature authorized spending another $2 million for military purposes. Meanwhile, many counties in the Old Dominion were appropriating local funds to help prepare their citizens for war. Overall, Virginia by the spring of 1861 was far better prepared for war than was any other Southern state. "Virginia," wrote Allan Nevins, "was foremost in effective preparation."

The Old Dominion's chief executive, John Letcher, whom Douglas Southall Freeman described as "a bald-headed, florid, bottle-nosed lawyer. . . . Not a brilliant man, [but] . . . level-headed," had opposed secession, but when it became evident that his state would leave the Union, he threw himself energetically into preparing its defense. On 23 April he appointed Robert E. Lee as a major general in the state army and put him in charge of all of Virginia's military resources.

Lee was, in the spring of 1861, a respected, distinguished officer who had spent his entire adult life in the United States Army. Lee and Letcher made an excellent team. The governor was a man of great common sense and impeccable honesty, and he had, according to his biographer, "unlimited confidence" in Lee. Letcher, therefore, allowed Lee to direct the state's military preparations without serious interference. For the next seven weeks—until the Virginia forces passed under Confederate authority on 8 June—Lee controlled the mobilization, organization, training, and deployment of his state's troops, guns, and even naval personnel.[2]

Tennessee had abolished her militia several years before the war, and as late as January 1861, her governor, Isham G. Harris, reported that there was no military force subject to the control of the state government. During the first half of 1861, Harris, a fanatical secessionist, was compelled to devote most of his time and energy to a desperate and ultimately successful effort to drag his state out of the Union and into the Confederacy. At the same time, he had to labor energetically to create a state military force that incorporated volunteer units organized by secessionists with other troops, including a reorganized militia, then being raised by the state.

On 6 May, the day the Tennessee legislature adopted the state's Declaration of Independence, it also passed a bill creating a fifty-five-thousand-man state army (twenty-five thousand for active duty; thirty thousand in the reserves). Three days later Harris named his political crony Gideon J. Pillow as the major general to command the Tennessee state army. Over the next five months Harris and Pillow organized and deployed the Tennessee state forces.

Pillow, therefore, did not formally begin to work with his state's military until more than two weeks after Lee had taken command in Virginia. Pillow's appointment was widely hailed in the press. On 10 May, for example, the *Nashville Union and American* called him "confessedly the first military man in experience and rank in the State"—a remark that, if true, goes a long way to account for the differences between the Army of Northern Virginia and the Army of Tennessee.

Such fulsome praise was typical of the way most Southern newspapers hailed all newly appointed Rebel generals. The truth was that Pillow, although possessed of some political and organizational skill, was a man of but slight military ability and—as it turned out—little physical and virtually no moral courage. At Fort Donelson, in February 1862, Pillow abdicated his command responsibilities and fled, leaving most of his men to be taken off to prisoner-of-war camps in the North. At Murfreesboro, on 2 January 1863, he hid behind a tree rather than go with his brigade into a charge against a strong Yankee position. He was, writes the historian William C. Davis, "a simple coward."

An Englishman who met Pillow in 1861 noted that he was "a small, compact, clear-complexioned man, with short grey whiskers, cut in the English fashion, a quick eye, and a pompous manner of speech." Pillow had been appointed a general in the Mexican War only because his political crony, James K. Polk, was then president of the United States, and in 1861 he still limped from a wound that he had received in that conflict.

In Mexico, so a widespread story had it, Pillow once ordered his men to entrench a position and to pile the dirt behind them rather than using it to build a protective breastwork in front of the trench. Lieutenant Ambrose Powell Hill, who knew him in Mexico, wrote in 1848 that "Pillow is as soft as his name and will no doubt be dismissed from the Army for barefaced lying." "Pillow," wrote Ulysses S. Grant in the 1880s, "was conceited, and prided himself much on his services in the Mexican War." In truth, Pillow's record in Mexico was undistinguished at best and marred by a bitter quarrel with his superior officer. Pillow, however, a vain, petty, and incompetent general, was convinced by his experiences in Mexico that he was a veritable military genius.[3]

DURING the short period that he was in command of the Virginia state army, Lee was concerned with the raising, organization, officering, equipping, and deployment of the Old Domin-

ion's military force. Although Lee faced many formidable problems during those seven weeks, he was blessed with far more
military resources, far better help, far more equipment, and a
much stronger foundation upon which to build than was his
Tennessee counterpart. Lee, for example, could build the Virginia army upon what his greatest biographer, Douglas Southall
Freeman, described as a "partly organized" militia of some
143,155 officers and men. This force included five regiments of
cavalrymen (many of whom were not armed), and, in addition,
there were some 12,000 organized volunteers in the state, including twelve companies of volunteer field artillery.

Virginia was far better provided with weapons for her troops
than was any other Confederate state. Virginians captured 1,198
heavy guns when they took possession of the United States Navy
Yard at Norfolk shortly after the state seceded. Although several
hundred of these guns were eventually shipped off to other Rebel
states for coastal and river fortifications, the haul furnished the
Old Dominion with more than an adequate number of heavy
guns for her own defense. At the time of secession, Virginia had
in storage in her own arsenals at Richmond and Lexington more
than 60,000 small arms. Even though about 90 percent of these
weapons were obsolescent flintlock muskets, their presence in
the state did mean that the Old Dominion was able to meet every
weapons requisition from Virginia troops and also to furnish
more than 10,000 muskets to troops from other states who were
sent to Virginia. Some 1,000 additional muskets from North
Carolina were sent to Virginia, and the spoils the Old Dominion
seized from the Federal posts in her borders also included
300,000 pounds of powder taken in Norfolk as well as 5,000
muskets and the invaluable gun-making machinery from the
United States arsenal at Harpers Ferry.

As the Virginia troops were organized and armed, Lee posted
them to protect the state and tried to see to it that they were
provided with competent commanders and trained as well as
possible. (For the officering and training, see Chapter 6.) Given
virtually a free hand by Letcher, Lee assigned the Virginia forces

to defend all the invasion routes along which the Old Dominion was threatened. From Norfolk in the southeastern part of the state across northern Virginia to Harpers Ferry and on through the mountainous area that later became West Virginia, military camps came into existence. The countryside of the Old Dominion resounded to the roll of drums, the shouted commands of drillmasters, and the grunts and curses of men as they worked to pull heavy guns into position.[4]

The late spring and early summer of 1861 witnessed quite a different scene in Tennessee. There was no Federal military installation in the state so local secessionists could not supply themselves with weapons from that source. The state armory in Nashville contained only about 8,000 flintlock muskets along with a few other arms. Some of these weapons had been in storage since 1808, and almost all of them were damaged to a greater or lesser extent. The state's artillery consisted of exactly four guns—an old, unserviceable six-pounder iron gun, a damaged twelve-pounder bronze gun, and a pair of obsolescent six-pounders.

There was even more confusion than usual in the hasty organization of the Tennessee state army. Men were plentiful, but supply and administrative problems quickly arose to plague the war effort. The Confederate government sent a few arms to the state but stipulated that they could be issued only to Tennessee regiments that were in Confederate (not Tennessee) service. Nine of the first regiments from Tennessee that did go into Confederate service were promptly armed and then ordered off to the Virginia front by the Rebel War Department. Many Tennesseeans, as they became aware of Rebel policy, refused to go into Confederate service. Others refused to leave the state; still others would not serve at all unless they were issued the same equipment that had been given to the troops leaving for Virginia. In the late spring of 1861, writes the historian of the Volunteer State's military force, the Rebel units in Tennessee "consisted of state regiments that refused to leave the borders of the state, regiments which were willing to join the Confederate army under any circumstances, Confederate regiments [organized in Tennessee and] . . . promptly shipped elsewhere, and state regiments which would have gladly entered Confederate service if arms had been made available." Only gradually was the confusion lessened and weapons procured.

While the eager new soldiers were pouring into the Tennessee camps of instruction, Harris and Pillow—left without any supervision for several months—had to deploy their troops. They elected to station most of the Tennessee units to defend the state's western border along the Mississippi River. In part, this inept deployment resulted from Harris's naive belief that Kentucky, as either a Confederate or a neutral state, would shield the northern border of Tennessee from invasion. The decision was also made to help relieve the widespread popular fear that the greatest danger to the Volunteer State would come from a Federal thrust down the Mississippi. This fear, in turn, was largely the product of both the propaganda that Harris had used to frighten the public into supporting secession and the fact that Northern officials were then known to be considering Scott's "Anaconda plan," which had as its centerpiece an effort to split the Confederacy along the line of the Mississippi. Harris's decision also grew from Tennessee politics. The governor was running for reelection in the summer of 1861, and he did not want to generate anger among the antisecessionist voters of East Tennessee by stationing large numbers of Rebel troops in their midst until after the 8 August voting.

In June 1861 Harris and Pillow had fifteen thousand men stationed in forts along the Mississippi River, and Pillow had established his headquarters in the famous Gayoso House in Memphis—a poor location for a general who was responsible for the defense of the entire state. It is questionable, furthermore, whether Pillow's river defenses would have been very effective (they were never seriously tested). At Memphis, for example, Pillow constructed his fortifications directly on the edge of a high bluff that rose almost perpendicularly from the river. As the visiting English journalist William H. Russell observed, a Yankee gunboat could easily have tumbled the entire system of works into the water simply by firing a few shells into the bluff underneath the Rebel positions.

Pillow and Harris assigned fewer than four thousand troops to protect Middle Tennessee and sent only a token force to East Tennessee. This poor allocation of manpower led directly to a failure to defend adequately the Tennessee and Cumberland rivers and East Tennessee. That failure, in turn, was to cost the Confederacy dearly in the winter of 1861–62, when the Federals struck at and broke the left center and right rather than the left of the grossly unbalanced defensive line that Harris and Pillow had been responsible for establishing to protect their state.[5]

THE manner in which the state military forces of Virginia and Tennessee were transferred to Confederate control also differed radically. On 7 May Letcher directed Lee to take charge of all Southern troops in Virginia until and unless Confederate President Jefferson Davis should order otherwise. Three days later, Rebel Secretary of War Leroy P. Walker confirmed Lee's authority over all Confederate forces in Virginia. As troops from the Deep South reached the Old Dominion, they came immediately under the direction of a competent general who deployed them in conjunction with the state forces. The merger of the Virginia troops into the Confederate army went smoothly and was completed early. In the late summer of 1861, Virginia abandoned her attempt to maintain a separate state army on active duty. Her military-age volunteers went into the state's regiments in Confederate service. Men who chose not to volunteer remained in the militia and could be called for duty in an emergency. After the spring of 1862 they fell under the Confederate conscription laws and could be drafted for active duty in the Rebel army.[6]

The Tennessee state army, by contrast, was not formally placed under Confederate authority until 31 July 1861. The actual transfer progressed very slowly, and it was not until the end of October that all of the Volunteer State's army had legally been turned over to the Confederate government. Even as late as

January 1862, there was some confusion about whether the state or the Confederate government controlled the appointment of officers in some of the Tennessee units.[7]

When Confederate military authority was finally established in Tennessee, it was done piecemeal and in a manner that often exacerbated existing problems. On 13 July Leonidas Polk, holding the newly created grade of major general in the Southern army, assumed command of what the Confederate government chose to designate as Department Number 2. This territorial command extended northward along the Mississipi River from the thirty-first parallel (the northern boundary of East Louisiana) in a narrow strip that included Arkansas east of the White River and Tennessee west of the Cumberland River. (Department Number 1 was the lower Mississippi Valley.)

Polk thus brought West Tennessee and the military units stationed there under Confederate control. He came, moreover, to the area of the state that was assumed to be in the greatest danger. With his authority over Tennessee limited to the far western part of the state and with his headquarters in Memphis, it is not surprising that Polk, like the state officials before him, came to place an exaggerated emphasis on the supposed threat from up the Mississippi.

Not until September was the remainder of Tennessee brought into the Western Department, and by then local political pressure to protect West Tennessee had grown too great to permit a correction of the poor deployment of troops that had been made by Harris and Pillow in the preceding spring. Nor did the Confederate government, isolated in distant Richmond and mesmerized by the events in Virginia, put much emphasis on the organization of the Rebel defenses in Tennessee.[8]

BY far the most striking—and probably the most long-lasting— difference between the Virginia and the Tennessee state armies was in the attitude of their respective commanders toward the establishment of Confederate authority over themselves and their forces. On 23 April, after Virginia's secession, Lee learned that Confederate authorities were fearful that he, a state major general, would be offended at being made subject to the command of a Confederate brigadier general (then the highest grade in the Rebels' national army). Such a brouhaha might lead the Virginia State Convention to refuse approval of a then-pending agreement for military cooperation between the Old Dominion and the Confederacy.

Appreciating the absolute necessity for unity and cooperation in wartime, Lee hastened to assure Confederate officials that they should not consider his personal situation in making their decisions. He told Confederate Vice-President Alexander H. Stephens "that he did not wish anything connected with himself individually or his official rank, or *personal* position to interfere in the slightest degree" with having the Virginia forces pass under Confederate control as soon as possible. On 14 May Lee became a brigadier general in the Confederate army.

In contrast to Lee, the "vain and overstuffed" Pillow protested when he learned that he would lose control of the Tennessee troops and become a brigadier general in the Confederate army. Pillow argued that the Tennessee state force should be withheld from Confederate control unless its separate organization could be preserved and its officers retain the grades they had held in state service.

When he was overruled, Pillow entered the Confederate army resenting his demotion—a resentment that festered beneath the surface and ultimately "left an open wound" in the high command of what became the Army of Tennessee. Pillow, who "found it difficult to be second in power to anyone," fumed when he was placed under Polk's orders after that general assumed command in West Tennessee. The two men quickly fell to arguing over a proposed Rebel offensive into Missouri. The bitter quarrel that ensued consumed the two men's time and energies, diverted them from their real problems, divided and seriously hampered the western Confederates during the first year of the war, and set a dangerous and fatal precedent of bitter personal feuding among the generals of the Army of Tennessee. The editor of the Little Rock *Arkansas State Gazette* was not wrong when he wrote: "We know Gen. Pillow of old, and his ignorance, inefficiency, and general disqualification for Military command, are only equalled by his perverseness as an insubordinate and pestilent mischief maker. His appointment was a mistake which can only be remedied by striking his name from the roll of Confederate generals."[9]

I N their embryonic stages both the Army of Northern Virginia and the Army of Tennessee formed around the nucleus of existing state forces. Both armies were commanded by state major generals, and both were well organized, for Harris and Pillow, despite their egregious blunders of strategy and Pillow's personal shortcomings, did eventually get the Tennessee state forces organized on a reasonably sound footing. The early differences between the two armies were to be found in the degree of each state's preparation for war, in the way each state army came under Confederate control, and, most important, in the legacy each state army bequeathed to its successor.

The Letcher-Lee bequest was the wise use of manpower resources and a spirit of cooperation with the Confederate government. The Harris-Pillow legacy, by contrast, was the foolish deployment of resources and personal pettiness and rancor on the part of a general who put his own status ahead of his country's welfare and the welfare of the men entrusted to his command.

In summary, Letcher was a better war governor than Harris, and Lee was a better army commander and a much greater man than Pillow. The legacies of the two state armies determined much of the wartime—and hence the historiographical—fate of both the Army of Northern Virginia and the Army of Tennessee long before either of the two great Rebel armies had ever fired a shot in support of the Southern cause.

CHAPTER SIX

Officers and Enlisted Men

All through the first year of the war military units from the other Confederate states poured into Virginia and Tennessee. Once arrived on the Confederacy's northern frontier, these troops joined with the units of Lee's and Pillow's forces to form the two major armies of the South. After these two armies came into existence, it quickly became obvious that they were differentiated by factors other than their history.

Common sense, politics, geography, and logistics all combined to dictate that the Confederate authorities usually sent a unit to serve with a military force close to its home. To send Texas units to defend the North Carolina coast and rush Tarheel troops west to protect the frontier against Indians would have placed an unnecessary burden on the South's fragile transportation system and subjected government officials to well-founded criticism for waste, inefficiency, and needlessly separating soldiers from their home folk. In some cases, moreover, such a policy would also have exposed many troops unnecessarily to a climate to which they were not accustomed and to diseases against which they had no immunity.

The decision to assign most troops to armies close to their homes was, therefore, rational, but it had the incidental side effect of making the Army of Tennessee a western army and the Army of Northern Virginia an eastern army. In so doing, the decision contributed in two ways to the different fates of the two great Rebel armies.

The East-West differences can easily be seen by examining the organization of the two armies at several dates during the war. (For purposes of this analysis, the states and the military units from them are classified into the same groups that were used for the discussion of economic data in Chapter 2 with the addition of Maryland, Kentucky, Missouri, and the Confederate government as noted. Maryland, Virginia, and the Carolinas were the eastern Confederate states. The western Rebel states were Missouri, Kentucky, Tennessee, Alabama, Mississippi, Louisiana, Arkansas, and Texas. Units from Georgia and Florida and those organized directly under the auspices of the Confederate government are listed as central states' units.)

At the time of the Seven Days' Battle in June 1862, the Army of Northern Virginia contained 275 units that bore state designations. These units included infantry and cavalry regiments and battalions, some independent companies, "legions," and artillery batteries. Of these units, 176 (64 percent) were eastern, 51 (18.5 percent) were western, and 48 (17.5 percent) were from the central South.

At about the same time, the Army of Tennessee, which was then operating in Mississippi, contained a total of 169 units. The western states of the Confederacy furnished 154 (91.1 percent) of the units then with the Army of Tennessee; the eastern states provided 2 units (1.2 percent; both from South Carolina); and the central states sent 4 units (2.4 percent). The designations of 9 units (5.3 percent) are unknown.

This pattern did not change significantly during the war, as the data in Tables 6.1 and 6.2 indicate.

These data make it clear that there were always far more western units serving in Virginia than there were eastern units with the Army of Tennessee. In the spring of 1862, for example, Alabama had seventeen units in Virginia—more than eight times the total number of eastern units then serving in the West. At the same time, Louisiana had fifteen units in the Virginia army and Mississippi had eleven. Even the tiny Virginia contingent of three infantry regiments from Texas was half again as large as the entire number of eastern units then with the Army of Tennessee.

On the four dates covered by this survey, Virginia had between 103 and 134 units serving with the Army of Northern Virginia; she never had more than 3 assigned to the Army of Tennessee. In

TABLE 6.1

Geographical Distribution of Units in the Army of Northern Virginia

Date	Total Units	Eastern Units	Central Units	Western Units
Late 1862	271	167 (61.6%)	52 (19.5%)	52 (19.5%)
Fall 1863	322	215 (66.4%)	50 (15.5%)	57 (17.6%)
Spring 1864	351	232 (66.1%)	57 (16.2%)	62 (17.7%)

fall of 1863 Tennessee furnished 62 units to the Army of Tennessee and only 3 to the Army of Northern Virginia. North Carolina was represented in the Virginia army by between 38 and 65 units; she never had more than 9 with the Army of Tennessee. South Carolina had between 20 and 31 units serving in Virginia but not more than 6 in the West.

The historian Robert Krick calculates that a total of 385 infantry, cavalry, and artillery units of battalion size or larger served with the Army of Northern Virginia at some time during the war. The Old Dominion furnished 148 of those units (38.4 percent). The eastern Rebel states sent a total of 256 units (66.5 percent) to Lee's army. Sixty-four units (16.6 percent) went from the central Confederate states to the Virginia army and 65 (16.9 percent) from the western states. Unfortunately, no one has compiled a similar list for the Army of Tennessee. At any one time about two-thirds of the Army of Northern Virginia's units hailed from the eastern states of the Confederacy; about three-fourths of the troops in the Army of Tennessee were from the West.

That so many western units were sent to the East yet so few eastern units served in the West was more the result of demographics than of any deliberate plan. The eastern Rebel states had only 37 percent of the Confederacy's white population; the western states had 50.1 percent. The Southerners relied on the eastern states to provide most of the troops for the Virginia army, but it was not possible for that region alone to furnish

Two Great Rebel Armies

TABLE 6.2

Geographical Distribution of Units in the Army of Tennessee

Date	Total Units	Eastern Units	Central Units	Western Units
Late 1862	175	13 (7.4%)	34 (19.4%)	128 (73.1%)
Fall 1863	218	13 (6%)	37 (17%)	168 (77.1%)
Spring 1864	277	13 (4.7%)	49 (17.7%)	215 (77.6%)

enough men to keep the Army of Northern Virginia at the desired strength. The West, with its larger population, could furnish enough men for the Army of Tennessee and have some left over to send to Virginia for service on the eastern front.[1]

UNLESS one posits the existence of a pool of militarily deficient genes in the western states of the Confederacy, these differences in the geographical origins of the rank and file of the two most important Southern armies are of no direct importance in explaining the differences in their records. Certainly there is nothing in Civil War history to suggest that troops from the western Confederacy were any less brave and skillful than their eastern comrades. Richard Taylor's fine Louisiana brigade, the magnificent Alabama troops brought to Virginia by Evander Law and Robert E. Rodes, Hood's Texas Brigade, the Washington Artillery of New Orleans, the Third Arkansas Regiment, and other units in the Army of Northern Virginia were all proof of the military prowess of the western Rebels. Nor can anyone who studies the 30 November 1864 Battle of Franklin, Tennessee, and goes over that terrible field have any doubt that the enlisted men of the Army of Tennessee were at least as courageous as their counterparts who fought in Virginia.

Although of no importance for the rank and file, the differences in the geographical origins of the two major Confederate armies did influence their histories and, therefore, the course of the war. The very large Virginia contingent in the Army of Northern Virginia—at times over 40 percent of the eastern army consisted of units from the Old Dominion—could only have strengthened the degree to which that army was identified in both North and South with the heroic, mythical Virginia cavaliers. Conversely, the all but total absence of Virginians from the Army of Tennessee deprived the western Confederates of a great deal of the mythical aura that surrounded the Rebels' eastern army. In September 1863, when the western Confederate army finally won a major victory, it did so only with the help of reinforcements sent from the Army of Northern Virginia. Such factors inevitably affected—in different ways—the morale and esprit de corps of both Yankees and Rebels in both East and West.

The second way in which geographical differences influenced the two armies was much less obvious but far more important. This second difference stemmed from the way the Confederates raised and trained their armies. Almost all of the regiments in Rebel military service were raised by the individual state governments. Usually some locally prominent citizen would take the lead in organizing a company in his town or county. A public meeting would be convened at which the audience would be treated to stirring speeches, patriotic music, and good food. After the young men in the audience were in the proper mood, the "muster books" would be opened, and all who desired to enlist were invited to come forward and enroll their names.

Once the company had secured its full complement of men (about one hundred, depending upon the type of unit), it would hold an election for its captain, the junior officers, and the noncommissioned officers, adopt a name (for example, the Mississippi Yankee Hunters), and set about trying to master the business of becoming soldiers. After these steps had been taken, the captain would formally offer the company's services to the governor. When the governor accepted the offer, he would order the captain to move his command to one of the state-operated camps of instruction, where it would undergo further training. At the camp, the company was combined with nine other companies to form a regiment.

At this point the company would be designated by letter and the regiment by number and state name. The Mississippi Yankee Hunters, for example, became Company K, First Mississippi Infantry Regiment. The regiment's officers were usually elected, either by vote of the entire regiment or by the officers of the regiment's companies. (In some cases the governor was able to appoint the regimental officers, and there was a rarely used provision in Confederate law under which the president, in certain circumstances, was empowered to name the officers of a few regiments.) When the Confederate War Department called upon the state for troops, the governor would order the regiment to proceed to the "seat of war" as part of the state's quota. For most Rebel units the seat of war was in either Virginia or Tennessee—by and large the former for eastern regiments, the latter for most of the western units.

This method of raising the Confederate army—and troops were raised in much the same way in the North—meant that the quality of a state's regiments, especially in the crucial early months of the war, was to a very great extent the direct result of that state's ability to provide competent, knowledgeable company and regimental officers and noncommissioned officers to train the thousands of raw recruits who were pouring into the army in the first flush of military enthusiasm. There were only a few men in Civil War America who were qualified to offer such instruction to new troops. Bruce Catton wrote that most Northern officers in 1861 "knew no more about military matters than the recruits they were supposed to instruct" and that there were "hardly any men who knew how to do the teaching" of new soldiers.

Catton's statement is equally applicable to most of the Confederacy. Nevertheless, a state that was able to provide a significant number of men who were qualified to instruct the raw, young soldiers in the arcane intricacies of company and regimental drill and the complex nineteenth-century manual of arms would, all other things being equal, provide better-trained—and hence more effective—units than could states whose officers and sergeants had to learn the drills as they were trying to teach them to their men.[2]

There were three sources from which a Confederate state could quickly obtain men with military experience who were qualified to train its troops. Men who had served in the United States Army, Navy, or Marine Corps, or in the armed forces of some other nation, constituted a valuable source of readily available military knowledge and experience. This category included both men who were on active duty at the time their state seceded and men who had left the service and taken up some civilian occupation before the Civil War. Service with the militia or with one of the volunteer units provided a second source of men with at least some martial knowledge and experience. The third group consisted of men who had been educated at a state or private military school but who had never been on active military duty.

Many men, of course, came to Confederate service with experience in two of these categories. Owing both to its geographical roots in the eastern Rebel states and to the manner in which Confederate troops were raised and trained, the Army of Northern Virginia—especially the regiments from the Old Dominion—contained a far higher number of officers, noncommissioned officers, and even privates who had had some military experience before 1861 than did the Army of Tennessee.

There are no complete statistical data to prove that far more men with prewar military experience served in the Rebels' eastern army, but the partial data that are available leave no room for doubt. Douglas Southall Freeman calculated that in 1861, Virginia could claim a total of 104 living graduates of the United States Military Academy; the other ten Confederate states had a combined total of only 184. In early 1861 an officer in Nashville, Tennessee, made a compilation of the 1,132 officers then on active duty with the United States Army. He found that 304 of them were from the eleven states that were eventually to join the Confederacy. Of these 304 officers, Virginia was credited with

137, South Carolina with 40, and North Carolina with 36—a total of 213 (70.1 percent) from the three eastern Confederate states. Another 36 of these officers (11.8 percent) hailed from Georgia and Florida. Only 55 (18.1 percent) were from the six western Confederate states—just two-fifths of the number from Virginia alone.[3]

Almost all of the active duty officers who left the United States Army in 1860–61 to go with the South went to their home states and entered military service as members of state units. The seceded states that had sent large numbers of men into the officer corps of the antebellum United States Army therefore experienced an influx of former regular army officers most of whom spent the early months of their Civil War service training some of their home states' newly organized regiments. Lewis A. Armistead left the United States Army and became colonel of the Fifty-seventh Virginia before he was promoted to brigadier general. Jeb Stuart returned to the Old Dominion and spent several months training the First Virginia Cavalry. After Stuart was promoted to brigadier general, the regiment was commanded successively by W. E. "Grumble" Jones and Fitzhugh Lee—two other West Pointers. Ambrose Powell Hill commanded the Thirteenth Virginia for almost a year. Charles W. Field served as colonel of the Sixth Virginia Cavalry. Stephen Dodson Ramseur left the old army and took command first of a North Carolina artillery battery and then of the Forty-ninth North Carolina. William Dorsey Pender, another Tarheel officer who resigned from the Federal army in 1861 to go with his state, entered Confederate service as colonel of the Thirteenth North Carolina.

Similar assignments took place all over the eastern Confederacy in the spring of 1861 as regular officers resigned from the United States Army and returned to their homes. All through the eastern camps of instruction these experienced officers were able to apply their knowledge to the training of the newly raised regiments. Fewer officers were from the western Confederate states, and consequently fewer were available to train the Rebel units raised in the West.

The supply of experienced officers was even more concentrated in the Army of Northern Virginia than the above data and examples indicate. Many western regiments were sent to Virginia to serve in the eastern army. Many of the recently resigned officers from the United States Army whose homes were in the western Confederacy, therefore, spent the early part of the war as field grade officers (colonels, lieutenant colonels, and majors) in the Army of Northern Virginia. Cadmus M. Wilcox of Tennessee served for several months before his promotion to brigadier general as colonel of the Ninth Alabama in the Virginia army. John Bell Hood, born in Kentucky but to gain fame in Rebel service as a Texan, made the Fourth Texas Infantry into one of the best combat units in the Army of Northern Virginia—indeed, in the entire Confederacy. John Pelham of Alabama withdrew from the United States Military Academy when his state seceded and compiled a distinguished record in the artillery of the eastern army. If there was more than one former United States Army officer from an eastern Confederate state who resigned in 1861 and served as a field grade officer in the Army of Tennessee or its predecessor units, his name escapes me. The exception was John B. Villepigue of South Carolina, who left the old army in March 1861 and served for a while as colonel of the Thirty-sixth Georgia Infantry—a regiment that became part of the Army of Tennessee.[4]

HISTORIANS of the Civil War have usually treated the Confederate-era militias as something of a joke. The state militias are often thought of in conjunction with the song "Eatin' Goober Peas," and, if they are mentioned at all in the literature of the war, they are almost always dismissed as a serious factor in the conflict's military history. Often Civil War historians like to quote Sam Watkins on the Southern militia of the 1860s. Watkins, a self-styled "high private" in the First Tennessee Regiment, fought through most of the war with the western Confederate army. In the summer of 1864 the Georgia state militia was ordered to the field to assist the Army of Tennessee in the last stages of the Atlanta Campaign. Watkins wrote of the militiamen whom he saw marching to the front:

> Every one was dressed in citizen's clothing, and the very best they had at that time. A few had doubled-barreled shot guns, but the majority had umbrellas and walking-sticks, and nearly every one had on a duster, a flat-bosomed "biled" shirt, and a plug hat; and to make the thing more ridiculous, the dwarf and the giant were marching side by side; the knock-kneed by the side of the bow-legged; the driven-in by the side of the drawn-out; the pale and sallow dyspeptic . . . who seemed to have just been taken out of a chimney that smoked very badly, and whose dirt was goobers and sweet potatoes, was placed beside the three-hundred pounder, who was dressed up to kill.

The implication is clear: the militiamen were laughingstocks as soldiers, and they made no real contribution to the Confederacy's military effort. Watkins's comment, even if true—and one must always be careful about accepting any postwar statements as completely accurate—applied only to the militiamen he saw in 1864. By that time, virtually all able-bodied white male Southerners of military age were in active Confederate service, and the militia was to a great extent a collection of the young, the old, and the lame. The militia of 1861, at least in those states that took a serious interest in their own defense, was a different type of military force.

The militia, in fact, did contribute in three ways to the Southern cause. Two of these contributions stemmed from the militia's traditional role of providing an organized body of trained men who, in an emergency, could be called as a unit to active duty. Such units could be used to guard prisoners, supplies, bridges, and trains and to perform other noncombat duties. By so doing, the militiamen freed Confederate veterans to return to their units in the front lines. Second, militia units, if well handled and used in the appropriate circumstances, could be of much assistance in active operations. Even Watkins noted of the 1864 Georgia militiamen that "there was many a gallant and noble fellow among them" and related the story of a patrol on which the militia had helped to capture some Yankees. Militiamen were usually far better at defending a position—especially a fortified position—as they did at Honey Hill, South Carolina, on 30 November 1864 than they were at attacking the enemy, as they tried and failed to do at Griswoldville, Georgia, on 22 November 1864, when they were slaughtered.

It was through the third, indirect, and least visible of their roles, however, that the Southern state militias made their greatest contribution to the Rebel cause. In addition to providing fully organized units, the militia, from its earliest days in the colonial period, had also served as a manpower pool from which trained individuals could be drawn for active service with regular or especially organized active duty units. The militia thus served to give citizens some military training. To the extent that a Confederate state had kept up its militia force in the antebellum years, it had in 1861 a body of at least partially trained men from which it could raise its quota of troops to send to the Rebel army. Even more important, it had a group of men who had acquired some experience as officers in small unit drill, tactics, and administration.

We do not know a great deal about the 1861 militias of the Confederate states. The militiamen often appear in the records as shadowy figures who were hastily called to duty by the governors early in 1861 to help seize Federal military installations in each state as it seceded. Soon afterward their units were released from duty and sent home—usually to be replaced by newly raised regiments in Confederate service—and most of the militiamen themselves volunteered as individuals for one of the quickly organized companies that was preparing to rush off to do battle with the Yankees. What we do know, however, indicates that Virginia was able to draw from her militia far more men with at least some military knowledge and experience than was any other Rebel state.

In late 1860 the Old Dominion's militia was organized into

187 regiments of infantry (1,214 companies), with 5,393 officers and 132,917 enlisted men. There were also 5 regiments of cavalry, numbering 207 officers and 3,572 enlisted men, as well as 5 regiments of artillery (17 companies) with 70 officers and 996 enlisted men. The total strength was 143,155 officers and men. These figures are from a report, "Militia of the United States," compiled by the War Department for the Thirty-seventh Congress. Unfortunately, at the time the report was compiled, the information for the other Southern states was so out of date as to make comparisons with Virginia meaningless. The other returns—presumably the latest available data—ranged from 1838 for Mississippi to 1859 for Louisiana and Arkansas, which may, by itself, tell us a great deal about the condition of the militias in those states.

In addition to its large manpower pool, the Old Dominion was reported to be in possession of 69 brass pieces of artillery and 221 iron artillery pieces. North Carolina was reported to have had a total of 15 cannon, South Carolina, 49. Only Arkansas among the western Rebel states was reported to have had any militia artillery at all—one howitzer.

When Virginia called her sons to active duty for Confederate service, she was able to draw from a large body of men who were far more likely to have learned something of military matters from duty with the militia. The Old Dominion's militia was no highly trained, fully armed, embryo Prussian military force, but its existence meant that Virginia had a far larger number of men with some military experience than did any of the other seceding states. Virtually all of these men performed their Confederate service in the Old Dominion.[5]

THE Army of Northern Virginia contained more former regular army and militia officers than did the Army of Tennessee, but it was from the Confederacy's third source of qualified leaders that the Rebels' eastern army derived a strength of command that gave it an even greater advantage over both its western counterpart and its eastern opponent. Men who had received both a college education and military training in school were present in far greater numbers in the Army of Northern Virginia than in any other Civil War military force. Their presence made that army a far better military organization than any of its American contemporaries.

Robert Krick, who has made a study of the field grade officers who served with the Army of Northern Virginia, calculates that 1,965 men served as colonels, lieutenant colonels, or majors in that army. (The total excludes men who were promoted to general officer and counts each man only in the highest grade that he held.) Of this total, calculates Krick, 156 were educated at the Virginia Military Institute, 73 at the United States Military Academy, 37 at the South Carolina Military Academy (the Citadel), 14 at the Georgia Military Institute, 4 at the United States Naval Academy, and 1 at LaGrange Military Academy.

The military schools, however, provided an even more valuable command resource than field grade officers. As Union Major General William T. Sherman observed in September 1864, "Good corporals and sergeants, and . . . good lieutenants and captains . . . are far more important than good generals." The military schools provided hundreds of such well-qualified junior officers and noncommissioned officers to the Army of Northern Virginia. No other Civil War army was so well supplied in 1861 with men capable of stepping immediately into junior command positions, training the new troops, and exercising effective leadership at the company level.[6]

There were military schools all over the South in 1861 as well as military programs at a number of other colleges and universities. In 1861, however, most of these schools and programs were small and of recent origin. VMI, founded in 1839, and the Citadel, established four years later, were by far the most important such schools in the Confederacy. Unfortunately, the Citadel has but few records of its pre–Civil War alumni. VMI records, on the other hand, are complete enough to yield a good picture of what that school meant to the Confederacy in general and to the Army of Northern Virginia in particular.

The V.M.I., as proper Virginians refer to the school, had been established in Lexington, where the cadets, as a part of their military training, were used to guard the state arsenal and the weapons stored there. By the summer of 1861, almost 1,000 cadets had enrolled at the institute, and 455 had been graduated. Almost all of the 523 who were not graduated had remained at the school for at least six months and had thus had a chance to learn the basics of soldier life. Only 35 of these 978 cadets came from outside Virginia (including what is now West Virginia). Seven of the outsiders were from Louisiana, 6 from North Carolina, and 5 from the District of Columbia. Only 3 were from the North (one each from Pennsylvania, New York, and Indiana).[7]

At VMI, the cadets received military training while they pursued their academic studies. New cadets reported to the institute in early July, and for about two months they and the old cadets lived in the field, undergoing what amounted to basic training. Often the Corps of Cadets staged marches through parts of the Shenandoah Valley. In the last decade before the war many of these marches took place under the direction of Major Thomas J. Jackson, an eccentric faculty member who was professor of natural and experimental philosophy and artillery tactics. After academic work resumed in the fall, the military training continued with daily guard mounts, sentry duty, inspections, parades, and drill.

In this environment the cadets became proficient in small unit drill, learned about hand and shoulder arms, and were given a great deal of valuable experience in small unit command, administration, and tactics. They learned to command and to obey. They drilled with artillery, using lightweight guns that had been especially cast for VMI when it was found that the regular cannon were too heavy to be pulled about by the freshmen (officially, "fourth classmen"—or, in VMI jargon, "rats"), who were harnessed to the pieces in lieu of horses.

When a cadet finished at VMI he had benefited from both excellent training in military matters and an education in a curriculum that stressed mathematics, science, engineering, and modern foreign languages. Only about two dozen VMI men went into the regular military service before 1861. Most became farmers, businessmen, engineers, editors, or teachers or went on for further schooling to become lawyers, doctors, or clergymen. The great majority of them remained in Virginia, where they settled down in their jobs and in raising their families. Many served as officers in local militia units.

When the Civil War began in the spring of 1861, VMI alumni, like their contemporaries North and South, were caught up in the excitement of mobilization. As of 1 July 1861 there were 882 living VMI alumni. Of these men, 740 are known to have served the Confederacy in some military or diplomatic capacity. Shortly after Virginia seceded, almost all of the cadets then enrolled at the institute were sent to the camps of instruction at Richmond to assist in training the newly organized units. Virtually all of these men then went directly into the Rebel army. In addition to the alumni and the 1861 corps, men from the large wartime classes left the institute all during the conflict to join the Confederate army. William Couper, the historian of VMI, calculated that a total of 1,796 VMI cadets and alumni were in Confederate service. Eighteen of these men became Rebel generals. Couper also believed that the institute furnished the Southern army with 95 colonels, 65 lieutenant colonels, 110 majors, 310 captains, and 221 lieutenants.[8]

What this reservoir of trained manpower meant to Virginia is well illustrated by the case of a company that was organized at Pierceville, Virginia, on 26 April 1861. After the men were assembled, the question of who could instruct them in the complicated maneuvers of the nineteenth-century drill arose. Dr. James McGavock Kent, who had attended VMI for about six months in 1840–41, was unanimously chosen as the captain, and the men began twice-a-day drill under his tutelage. This company, originally called the Bedford Letcher Greys, became Company F of the Twenty-eighth Virginia Infantry. Kent left the company in 1862 to become a Confederate surgeon, but the presence in the community of a citizen whose education had provided him with enough military knowledge and experience to train his comrades had proved to be of great value to the unit in its earliest days.

The Old Dominion sent fifty-six regiments and battalions of infantry and heavy artillery into Confederate service in the early months of the war. Twenty of them were commanded by VMI men. Two of the eight Virginia cavalry regiments organized in 1861 also began their service under the command of VMI alumni. Virtually every Virginia unit included several men who had studied at VMI. Some Old Dominion units had more than a dozen. John Mosby's famous Forty-third Battalion of Virginia Cavalry (Partisan Rangers) had about four dozen VMI men in its ranks. Thomas T. Munford's Second Virginia Cavalry had almost two dozen, and Munford himself was a member of the Institute's Class of 1852. Major General George E. Pickett's division—three brigades, fifteen Virginia regiments—was the spearhead of the great Confederate charge at Gettysburg on 3 July 1863. Thirteen of Pickett's regiments were commanded at some point in the charge by officers who were VMI alumni. In three of the regiments, both the colonel and the lieutenant colonel were VMI men.

Many of the VMI alumni who were living outside Virginia in 1861 also wound up fighting for the Confederacy in the Old Dominion in units from other states. Henry King Burgwyn, Jr., the "boy colonel" of the Confederacy, became commander of the Twenty-sixth North Carolina. He died at Gettysburg on 1 July 1863. William A. Forbes was, in 1861, president of Clarksville College in Tennessee. He returned to his native Virginia as colonel of the Fourteenth Tennessee and was mortally wounded at Second Manassas. Robert E. Rodes was living in Alabama when the war began. He helped raise and train the Fifth Alabama and brought that fine regiment to fight in Virginia. When he was killed at Winchester, Virginia, in September 1864, he was a major general. It has been estimated that more than 95 percent of the VMI men who held line (command of troop) positions—as well as a very high percentage of those who served as staff officers and engineers—served in Virginia units or in units from other states that became part of the Army of Northern Virginia.

On one (possibly apocryphal) occasion Abraham Lincoln was asked why it was taking so long for the large, well-equipped Federal armies to conquer the weaker Rebels. A Union victory over the Confederates, the president is supposed to have remarked, could be won much sooner "were it not for a certain military school they have which supplies them with trained officers." What Lincoln did not say—and did not know—was that virtually all of those trained officers were in the Army of Northern Virginia.[9]

Some three-quarters of a century after the Civil War, Douglas Southall Freeman, as he labored on his great work *Lee's Lieutenants: A Study in Command,* wrote: "In researches for my new book on the Confederacy, I have gone at considerable length into the part played by V. M. I. men and I am convinced that the Army of Northern Virginia owed to the Institute such excellence of regimental command as it had. I do not believe that the campaigns of 1862 could have been fought successfully without V. M. I. men." "The graduates of the Virginia Military Institute," writes Lee A. Wallace, Jr., "proved to be the greatest source for the state's potential officers.[10]

Education at a nineteenth-century state military school did not, in and of itself, qualify a young Southerner to be a great military commander or even a competent general, nor did it necessarily make him a qualified—or even a courageous—combat leader. Such an education, with its accompanying military training, however, did mean that most of the men who experienced it were well-prepared to serve as noncommissioned officers or as junior officers in 1861. States that had acted to provide themselves with such qualified men were able at the beginning of the war to field a cadre of instructors to train their newly organized regiments. The two Southern states that had done the most to make such provisions were Virginia and South Carolina, and the great majority of the alumni of their military schools—

virtually all in the case of Virginia—served in the Army of Northern Virginia.[11]

Although there would have been no difference between the courage or intelligence of eastern and western leaders, the concentration of qualified men in the eastern states of Rebeldom meant that the overall level of military knowledge, experience, and training—especially in the first year of the war—was far higher in the officer corps of the Army of Northern Virginia than it was in the Army of Tennessee. The officers' ability to perform their most important duty—the training of their men—was higher. The administration of their units was better.

Men who had been educated and trained at a military school entered Confederate service already knowledgeable about small unit administration, drill, tactics, weapons, and other matters. That knowledge allowed them, from the start, to give their companies, batteries, battalions, and regiments a higher tone, more thorough training, greater confidence, and better discipline than would have been the case if the leaders had had to learn their duties after assuming command.

Testifying before the Congressional Committee on the Conduct of the War in 1865, Federal Major General Joseph Hooker, who had fought Confederates in Virginia, Tennessee, and Georgia, offered the following observation on why it had been so difficult to defeat the Army of Northern Virginia:

> Our artillery had always been superior to that of the rebels, as was also our infantry, except in discipline, and that for reasons not necessary to mention, never did equal [that of] Lee's army. With a rank and file vastly inferior to our own, intellectually and physically, that army has, by discipline alone, acquired a character for steadiness and efficiency unsurpassed, in my judgment, in ancient or modern times. We have not been able to rival it, nor has there been any near approximation of it in the other rebel armies.[12]

The initial differences that resulted from the presence of a cadre of trained officers and noncommissioned officers in the

Army of Northern Virginia would have become less pronounced as experience taught surviving leaders in the Army of Tennessee much about the business of leading, training, and administering small units. Yet basic initial differences were long-lasting, and troops trained by a competent officer at the beginning of their military service felt his influence long after he had been promoted or killed.

When a line officer or noncommissioned officer in the Army of Tennessee was killed or incapacitated, his replacement would frequently have to start from the beginning to learn his new duties; in the Army of Northern Virginia, the loss of one trained leader often meant his replacement by another. Extensive study of the history and records of both of the two major Southern armies leads inexorably to the conclusion that the Virginia army was better managed than was the Army of Tennessee. The organization of the eastern army was tighter and more efficient, its administration was more thorough and more sound, and—above all—its discipline was better than that of the Army of Tennessee. Much of this difference was because so many of the younger officers, sergeants, and corporals in the Army of Northern Virginia knew from the start of their military service what they were doing and how to do it.

CHAPTER SEVEN

The General Officers

The same differences in geographical origins that made the Army of Tennessee western and the Army of Northern Virginia eastern also affected the general officer corps of the two major Confederate armies. The differences between the general officers of the two armies, however, were less pronounced than were those between the lower-ranking officers. Line and field grade officers were intrinsic to a particular regiment or battalion from which they derived their grade. Generals, on the other hand, could be assigned and reassigned to different commands at the pleasure of the president. They were, therefore, more mobile than their lower-ranking comrades, and they could usually be sent to serve wherever the Confederate authorities thought they were most needed.

Despite the greater mobility of the general officers, there was a tendency for generals from the eastern states of the Confederacy to serve in Virginia and for those in the Army of Tennessee to hail from the West. This tendency was especially marked in the lowest and largest general officer grade—brigadier general. New brigadiers were most often appointed from among an army's colonels. Since there were few eastern regiments, and hence few eastern colonels, in the Army of Tennessee, there were few easterners present in that army to receive promotions. The same factor worked, although to a lesser degree, to hold down the number of western brigadiers in the Army of Northern Virginia. Political pressure to have troops commanded by a general from their own state also worked to limit the number of "outside" brigadiers.

Ezra Warner has concluded that 425 men attained the three stars and wreath that served as the insignia of all Confederate

The General Officers

TABLE 7.1
Geographical Distribution of Confederate Generals

Grade	Eastern Confederacy	Central Confederacy	Western Confederacy*	Total
General	3	1	4	8
Lieutenant general	10	1	6	17
Major general	29	10	33	72
Brigadier general	115	42	171	328
Total	157	54	214	425

*Includes, in addition to the states listed in Chapter 6, the Indian Territory.

general officers. These men were distributed among the four general officer grades and the three geographic regions of the Confederacy, as indicated in Table 7.1.

In all grades of generals, Virginia furnished more officers than did any other Rebel state. The Old Dominion gave to the Confederacy a total of 79 generals (3 full generals, 5 lieutenant generals, 17 major generals, and 54 brigadiers). Virginia's total was almost twice the number provided by second-place Georgia, which furnished 42 (1 lieutenant general, 7 major generals, and 34 brigadiers). Third-place Tennessee produced 40 members of the Rebel general officer corps (2 lieutenant generals, 8 major generals, and 30 brigadiers).

If one multiplies the number of general officer grades (four) by the number of Confederate states other than Virginia (ten; or fourteen counting the Indian Territory, Kentucky, Maryland, and Missouri), one produces forty possible grade/state combinations of general officers (or sixty-four counting the non-Confederate areas that produced Rebel generals). In only six of these forty (or sixty-four) categories did any other Rebel state have more than half the number of generals of that grade than did Virginia. To the extent that general officers represented military ability (and there is some room for debate on the subject), the Rebels' strength was the Old Dominion.[1]

No complete statistical studies of Confederate general officers have been made, but a comparison of some of the general officers of the Army of Northern Virginia with those of the Army of Tennessee produces some interesting results and tells us a great deal about the leaders of the two armies. I have used the four dates that were used in Chapter 6 to sample the armies' regiments (spring 1862, late 1862, fall 1863, and spring 1864). In both armies on all of the selected dates the commanding generals and the corps commanders were all men who had been trained at the United States Military Academy and who, with two exceptions, had spent all of their adult lives in professional military service or closely related work. Braxton Bragg had left the army in the mid-1850s to manage his property in Louisiana. He returned to military service early in 1861. Leonidas Polk had resigned from the army six months after his 1827 graduation from West Point to become an Episcopal clergyman. He was appointed a major general in 1861 by his old friend Jefferson Davis and assigned to the Army of Tennessee. Since the army and corps commanders were comparable in their education and experience and since, in any case, there were too few of them to have a meaningful impact, they can be omitted from the statistical comparison.[2]

The statistical survey indicates that there was in the Virginia army a definite tendency to place men of military education and experience in general officer positions whenever possible. Throughout 1862, for example, all of the major generals serving in the Army of Northern Virginia were men who had been educated at West Point and who had been career officers in the United States Army. In the spring of 1863, eight of the nine major generals of infantry in the Virginia army were West Pointers, and the ninth, Robert E. Rodes, was a graduate of the Virginia Military Institute who had performed brilliantly in lower command positions. At the opening of the 1864 campaign, eight of the Virginia army's eleven major generals were West Point men, another (Rodes) was from VMI, and yet another (W. H. F. Lee) was a former officer of the United States Army although he had not been trained at a military school. Even after the attrition of three years of war, more than 90 percent of the major generals in the Army of Northern Virginia were men with extensive prewar military education, experience, or both.

The Army of Tennessee, with a much smaller pool of trained, experienced commanders to draw upon, began early in the war to assign nonprofessional officers as major generals. In the spring of 1862, three of the western army's eight major generals (Benjamin F. Cheatham, John C. Breckinridge, and Sterling Price) were prewar civilians (although each of them had had some prewar military service), who owed their positions in the army to factors other than military training and experience. By the opening of the 1864 campaign, only five of the eleven major generals in the Army of Tennessee were men with professional military education, although three others had been in regular military service before the war.

An examination of the brigadier generals reveals an even greater difference between the two armies. In the spring of 1862, 41.5 percent of the brigadier generals (17 of 41) in the Army of Northern Virginia lacked previous military experience; the Army of Tennessee had a comparable 44 percent (11 of 25). By the summer of 1863, the level of inexperienced brigadiers in the eastern army had risen to 58.1 percent (18 of 31). In the Army of Tennessee it was then 74.2 percent. As the final year of the war opened in the spring of 1864, the Army of Northern Virginia had men without prewar military experience in half of its brigadier general positions (22 of 44). At the same time, 69 percent of the brigadiers in the Army of Tennessee were from similar backgrounds.[3]

Unfortunately, the above data are not as clear-cut as the raw numbers might indicate. Many of the men who are classified as lacking prewar military experience had been in the antebellum militia or had served as volunteers in Mexico, the Seminole War, or the Texas War for Independence, or they had been involved with some military force in some capacity. The incomplete information that is available concerning their antebellum careers indicates that 294 of the Confederacy's 425 generals (69.2 percent) had had experience in some phase of military matters before 1861. Such experience ranged from enlisted service in the British army (Major General Patrick R. Cleburne of Arkansas), to study at the United States Naval Academy (Brigadier General George B. Hodge of Kentucky), to attendance at a military high school (Brigadier General William G. Lewis of North Carolina), to service as his father's military secretary (Lieutenant General Richard Taylor of Louisiana).

The proportion of generals who had had at least some prewar exposure to military life ranged from a high of 88.9 percent among Maryland's nine generals in gray to 50 percent for Alabama's thirty-four Rebel generals, to a low of zero for the one general from the Indian Territory. Here again, the eastern Confederacy produced a greater percentage of experienced generals, as the data in Tables 7.2 and 7.3 indicate.

The East-West difference becomes even more marked if one considers only the four states that, throughout the war, provided the bulk of the Army of Tennessee's manpower. Alabama, Georgia, Mississippi, and Tennessee gave the Confederacy a total of 145 generals; only 85 of them (58.6 percent) had had prewar military experience. This situation was a great deal more unbalanced than the simple raw numbers indicate because a large number of experienced men from the central and western states of the Confederacy served in the Virginia army. Brigadier Generals E. Porter Alexander of Georgia and Benjamin G. Humphreys of Mississippi, for example, were assigned to the Army of Northern Virginia.

No matter how the data are arranged, the conclusion is inescapable: the general officers of the Army of Northern Virginia were more likely to have had prewar military experience—and far more likely to have had the benefit of formal study of and training in military matters—than were their colleagues in the Army of Tennessee. With many exceptions—notably Nathan Bedford

TABLE 7.2

Confederate Generals with Known
Antebellum Military Experience

State	Total number of generals	Number (%) with military experience
Alabama	34	17 (50)
Arkansas	19	11 (57.9)
Florida	13	9 (69.2)
Georgia	42	28 (66.7)
Indian Territory	1	0 (0)
Kentucky	22	19 (86.4)
Louisiana	27	19 (70.4)
Maryland	9	8 (88.9)
Mississippi	29	17 (58.6)
Missouri	12	8 (66.7)
North Carolina	33	20 (60.6)
South Carolina	35	25 (71.4)
Tennessee	40	23 (57.5)
Texas	30	23 (76.7)
Virginia	79	67 (84.8)
Total	425	294 (69.2)

Forrest, John B. Gordon, and Wade Hampton—men without formal prewar military training and little or no prewar military experience would, other things being equal, perform less satisfactorily as generals than would men who had been so trained or who had had the benefit of some previous connection with the military.

As was the case with the field and company grade officers, such training and experience were especially valuable in the early months of the war, when officers were engaged in training their men to be soldiers and in the prosaic but essential tasks of

Two Great Rebel Armies

TABLE 7.3
*Confederate Generals with Known
Antebellum Military Experience,
Arranged by Region*

Region	Total number of generals	Number (%) with military experience
Eastern Confederacy	157	120 (76.4)
Central Confederacy	54	37 (68.5)
Western Confederacy	214	137 (64)
Total	425	294 (69.2)

routine administration so that a unit was fed, armed, and supplied as adequately as possible. In the performance of those tasks knowledge, training, and experience were invaluable.[4]

SOME of the differences between the general officer corps of the Confederacy's eastern and western armies naturally dated from the antebellum years, when the older and more populous slave states along the Atlantic seaboard furnished more officers to the United States Army than did their newer western sisters. Virginia and the Carolinas were sending men to West Point and into the United States military service while Texas was part of the Spanish Empire. Many of the differences, therefore, stemmed from the sheer number of trained officers available in the eastern Confederacy.

The difference also resulted from the character and quality of the individuals who were appointed to command in the state forces that were the nuclei of the two great Rebel armies. When the Virginia state army was organized in the spring of 1861, the secession convention directed the governor to "invite all efficient and worthy Virginians and residents of Virginia in the Army and Navy of the United States to retire therefrom and enter the service of Virginia." Old Dominion authorities from the first sought to secure the services of qualified officers, and they were very cautious about naming political figures without military experience to commands.

"Most of the appointments of general officers in the [Tennessee] state force," writes Thomas L. Connelly, "had been politically inspired." Governor Isham G. Harris sought to pay his political debts by rewarding some of his supporters with commissions as generals in the state army. In contrast to the Virginia officers, "few of the general officers of Harris' state army would distinguish themselves in Confederate service."[5]

Because of the better personnel resources available in the East and the emphasis on the appointment of qualified men as officers in the Virginia state army, the eastern army's high command was, on the whole, better than that of the Army of Tennessee. Even when the Army of Northern Virginia began to run low on West Pointers, it was able to draw on men from the Virginia Military Institute. By the time men without any formal prewar professional training were beginning to rise to high positions—Wade Hampton and John B. Gordon in 1864, for example—they had been officers for three years. In the Army of Tennessee, by contrast, such nonprofessionals as Benjamin F. Cheatham and John C. Breckinridge were major generals commanding divisions as early as the spring of 1862. Beginning in late 1863, such nonprofessionals as Cheatham, Breckinridge, and Thomas C. Hindman sometimes commanded corps in the Army of Tennessee. Not until the final year of the war did a nonprofessional, Wade Hampton, lead the Cavalry Corps of Lee's army; and it was December 1864 before a man with no formal prewar military training, John B. Gordon, commanded an infantry corps in the Army of Northern Virginia.

SOME of the personal characteristics of the eastern and western generals may, however, have contributed even more to the different fates of their armies than did any education, training, or experience the generals had undergone either before or during the war. Thomas L. Connelly, the historian of the Army of Tennessee, has described and evaluated many of the generals of that army. He regards most of them as miserable human and military specimens.

John C. Breckinridge, concludes Connelly, owed his promotion to major general "more to politics than ability," but his political connections (he was from Kentucky and had been vice-president of the United States from 1857 to 1861) made him "a useful propaganda instrument." Simon B. Buckner "mentally went to pieces" at Fort Donelson, Tennessee, in February 1862. George B. Crittenden was "hapless," and there were allegations that he drank too much. John B. Floyd was "a weak individual and given to indecision and lack of force in dealing with a subordinate." William J. Hardee was "a potential troublemaker" who "tended to criticize his superiors, yet shirked responsibility" himself. He was also possessed by "a love of army intrigue." Daniel Harvey Hill was "unpredictable," "inflexible," "uncompromising," "nervous, irritable . . . easily affronted," and he "seemed to provoke disputes with his fellow officers." John McCown was a "hot-tempered" officer who once called the Confederacy "a damned stinking cotton oligarchy." John Hunt Morgan was "always eager for public acclaim," and he sometimes ignored orders and took foolish risks in attempting to win it. Edmund Kirby Smith was "not a follower." He "burned with a mystical desire to redeem, to conquer," and he "had trouble listening to people." The "short, dapper, yellow-haired" Earl Van Dorn was "unsteady." He was also "flashy." Joseph Wheeler, the leader of the western army's cavalry, "evinced little ability in long-range planning" and often mishandled his assignments.

Perhaps the least admirable of all the subordinate western generals, however, was Leonidas Polk. According to Connelly, Polk "exhibited personality traits which would . . . prove injurious to the Army." He frequently treated his superiors "in a manner that smacked of insubordination" and "often chose to obey . . . only when it pleased him to do so." Polk had "a remarkable ability to evade the blame for situations that were the result of . . . flaws in his character." He was "stubborn," "childish," and "quarrelsome." He "relished petty quarrels" and possessed an "amazing—and irritating—ability . . . to emerge from a bungled operation with a minimum of criticism."

Although Connelly finds a few admirable leaders among the brigade and division commanders of the Army of Tennessee, he usually does not deal with those levels of command, and the reader of his books is left with the clear impression that the high command of the Rebels' western army was a kaleidoscopic collection of military misfits, incompetents, poltroons, stumble-bums, and buffoons, many of whom were too sick mentally or physically to be entrusted with soldiers' lives, too petulant to cooperate with each other or with their commander or with their government, and too petty to subordinate concern for their own place and status to their country's needs or to the welfare of their troops. They devoted more time and almost as much energy to quarreling among themselves as they did to fighting the Yankees, and when they did fight the Federals, their personal bickering often rendered them incapable of cooperation with each other and ensured the defeat of their army.[6]

By contrast, Douglas Southall Freeman, the greatest historian of the Army of Northern Virginia, found many "able officers" among Lee's lieutenants, and he wrote affectionately of "that company of gallant gentlemen" who led the corps, divisions, and brigades of the eastern army through four years of war. Although he admits that many of the eastern generals exhibited professional or personal shortcomings, Freeman made it clear that such deficiencies never reached paralyzing levels similar to those that Connelly describes among Confederate generals in the West.[7]

Such comments as those quoted above and others to follow in Chapter 8 tell us a great deal more about Connelly and Freeman and the respective times in which they lived and wrote than they do about the generals and the Confederate armies. Freeman lived in the last part of the nineteenth century and the first half of the twentieth. He was personally acquainted with many Rebel veterans, and he was thoroughly immersed in the myths and legends created by white Southerners in the decades after the war—myths in which all Confederates were portrayed as brave, admirable, heroic men to whom ultimate defeat came only because they were contending against overwhelming numbers and resources. Freeman would doubtless have subscribed to the injunction that if you can't say something good about a Confederate general, you shouldn't say anything at all.

Beyond question, Freeman's Virginia birth and his long association with Richmond—his family moved there from Lynchburg when he was five—helped to shape his outlook on the Civil War. Freeman's father, whom he much admired, was a veteran of the Army of Northern Virginia, and in 1925 the elder Freeman became the commander in chief of the United Confederate Veterans. The historian T. Harry Williams once remarked that Freeman was "a Virginia gentleman writing about a Virginia gentleman." Much of Freeman's greatest work, furthermore, was written in the 1930s and 1940s, when the United States faced the crises of the Great Depression and World War II. Heroic, gallant Confederates, who survived the crisis of the 1860s, could and did serve as fine examples for the Americans of those decades.

Connelly, on the other hand, grew up in Middle Tennessee, almost literally on the Nashville battlefield. Three of his great-grandfathers—so he was told by elderly relatives—had been privates in Nathan Bedford Forrest's cavalry. One deserted from the Rebel army. Connelly came to maturity in the second half of the twentieth century at a time when the "groves of academe" were permeated with a great deal of disillusionment and cynicism about the United States in general and about American heroes— especially military heroes—in particular. He lived in a late twentieth-century South that was moving rapidly away from many of the rose-hued myths of the late nineteenth century and in a time when few people, even among white Southerners, still venerated the Confederacy and its leaders.[8]

Even when one makes allowances for "presentism" in the writings of both of the leading historians of the two major Confederate armies, however, one is still left with the strong conviction that the generals of the Army of Northern Virginia, as a group, were more capable military commanders than were their counterparts in the Army of Tennessee. There was something beyond their personalities and their higher level of prewar military education, training, and experience that made the subordinate leaders of the eastern army better military commanders.

CHAPTER EIGHT

The Commanding Generals

One need not agree completely with Napoleon's dictum that "the general is the head, the whole of an army," to understand the ultimate difference between the Army of Northern Virginia and the Army of Tennessee. G. F. R. Henderson wrote of "a truth confirmed by the experience of successive ages, that a wise direction is of more avail than overwhelming numbers, sound strategy than the most perfect armament; a powerful will, invigorating all who come within its sphere than the spasmodic efforts of ill-regulated valour." "[An] army," he added, "is what its commander makes it; its character sooner or later becomes the reflex of his own; from him the officers take their tone; his energy or his inactivity, his firmness or vacillation, are rapidly communicated even to the lower ranks. . . . No army has ever achieved great things unless it has been well commanded. If the general be second-rate the army also will be second-rate."

Owing to the "notorious Confederate command system," which relied on the willingness of an officer to accomplish a task without specific instructions, the personality of the commanding general was, according to Thomas L. Connelly, especially crucial to Rebel military success. Thus the character of the commanding general and his ability to elicit the willing obedience and cooperation of his subordinates became the most important factor in determining whether his army succeeded or failed.

Despite all of the differences in the geographic areas where they campaigned and in their backgrounds, their histories, their origins, their organizations, and their personnel, the chief factor in explaining the different fates of the two major Confederate armies was to be found in the personality, character, intelligence, dedication, and, above all, in the integrity and moral courage of their commanding generals. "The Western armies of the Confederacy," wrote Henderson, "were led . . . by inferior men." "It was not the Army of Northern Virginia that saved Richmond," he commented, "but Lee." Nor, he might have added, was it the Army of Tennessee that lost the West but that army's commanding generals.[1]

FIVE men held command of the Army of Tennessee for significant lengths of time. All were educated at the United States Military Academy. All were, or had been for almost all of their adult lives, professional army officers; all were experienced soldiers and physically brave men. All of them would willingly have sacrificed their lives in the effort to win Confederate independence. One of them, in fact, did so, and two of the others were seriously wounded during the war. All of them have been described and evaluated by Thomas L. Connelly in his two-volume history of the Army of Tennessee.

The first commander of the Western Rebel army was Albert Sidney Johnston. Born in Kentucky in 1803, Johnston had been graduated from West Point in 1826, and he had served for many years in both the United States Army and the Texas army when that state was an independent republic. He had also been (1838–40) secretary of war of the Republic of Texas. When the Civil War began, Johnston was a brevet brigadier general in the United States Army and was in command of the Department of the Pacific with his headquarters in San Francisco. In May 1861, he resigned, and in the following month he set out on a long journey across the southwestern desert to join the Confederacy. In early September he reached Richmond, where he was hailed as a great military leader, received an appointment as a full general in the Rebel army, and was ordered to take command of all Confederate troops in the area stretching from the Alleghenies west to the Indian Territory (now Oklahoma).

Johnston arrived in Nashville in mid-September, conferred with Tennessee authorities, ordered troops to move northward to occupy Bowling Green, Kentucky, and set off on an inspection tour of the Confederate position at Columbus, Kentucky, on the Mississippi River. By mid-October Johnston had gone to Bowling Green, and he took personal command of the Southern forces there. For the next four months Johnston remained at Bowling Green, where he allowed himself to become increasingly trapped in the details of defending that post and therefore more and more isolated from the other parts of his far-flung command. With Johnston pretty much limiting his actions to those more suited to a post commander, there was no one to coordinate the activities of the western Rebels. Many facets of the western command were neglected, and when the Yankees broke through on the Tennessee and Cumberland rivers in February 1862, the entire Confederate line across southern Kentucky crumbled.

The collapse of the Kentucky line and Yankee control of the lower and middle stretches of the Cumberland and Tennessee rivers forced Johnston to abandon Nashville and West Tennessee. The scattered Confederate forces were finally pulled together in March at Corinth, Mississippi, where they were joined by reinforcements rushed northward from the Gulf Coast. By early April, the Confederates had gotten themselves reorganized, and Johnston led them out to attack the Union army, which was then encamped along the Tennessee River, a short distance northeast of Corinth. The ensuing Battle of Shiloh (6–7 April) was the Army of Tennessee's first great engagement. In the middle of the afternoon 6 April, Johnston was mortally wounded. He was then up on the front lines, directing—and sometimes leading—the movements of brigades and even of regiments.

According to Connelly, Johnston was a man whose "entire life [before the Civil War] had been frustrated." He was, Connelly writes, "never able to establish rapport with his sub-commanders." He had "an overly gentle nature and his childlike faith in human goodness brought him much grief." The naive Johnston was "an easy mark for an ambitious or insubordinate lieutenant" who wished to displace him as commander. Johnston "seemed able to grasp only one area of thought at a time, and unable to view the total command picture of his department." He was "a man easily swayed by subordinates." His administration of the army was poor; the strategic errors that he made were serious. His personality had many "weaknesses." His confidence "waned" in early 1862, and his "confused state of mind" and "bewilderment" hampered his control of the army. In this sorry and pitiable condition, he fell victim to the machinations of a wily and scheming subordinate and relinquished control over the army long before his death.[2]

The wily and scheming subordinate was Johnston's successor, General Pierre G. T. Beauregard. Born in Louisiana in 1818, Beauregard had been educated at West Point (Class of 1838) and had served in the United States Army until February 1861. He had commanded the Confederate forces that captured Fort Sumter in April 1861 and then had been sent to Virginia. He was at First Manassas on 21 July 1861, where he received much of the credit for the South's triumph in the first great battle of the war. In the months after Manassas, Beauregard fell into a bitter quarrel with President Jefferson Davis. In part, the quarrel grew from different ideas about how the Confederacy should conduct the war. Beauregard favored a concentration of Rebel forces and viewed as suicidal Davis's penchant for defending many far-flung points. In part, too, the bitterness grew from Beauregard's habit of complaining directly to his friends in the Confederate Congress—some of whom had served as his staff officers—about the failure of the Davis administration to provide what he regarded as adequate supplies for his army.

Beauregard also differed with the administration about some details of army organization, and he seems to have resented being placed second in command of the Rebel forces in Virginia. Beauregard's official report of the Battle of Manassas, submitted to the government in October 1861, also aroused the president's anger, as did a letter that the general published in the *Richmond Whig* on 7 November 1861. In both of these documents, the thin-skinned Davis thought, Beauregard tried to exalt himself at the expense of the president. By the late part of the year, political opposition to the Davis administration was building in the Confederate Congress and the Rebel press, and Beauregard was becoming identified with the movement.

At this juncture, in January 1862, through shenanigans that are not completely understood, the decision was made to transfer Beauregard to the West. The reassignment may have originated with some western congressmen who felt that Beauregard would help to provide stronger protection for their states. The administration may have hatched the idea as a way to rid itself of Beauregard, or some of the general's friends may have made the proposal to give him a chance to improve his fortunes in another area. Whatever the origin of the idea, President Davis agreed to the transfer if Beauregard would accept. The general, perhaps desiring a more active command and believing that he could return to his post in Virginia as soon as he had cleared up the problems in the Mississippi Valley, agreed to go. He thus became one of "that troubled set of officers sent to the West for varied purposes—none beneficial to the western army." He also came "under a cloud of governmental displeasure."

Beauregard reached Bowling Green in early February and soon took command of the seventeen thousand Confederate troops stationed about Columbus, Kentucky. Unfortunately for Beauregard, he arrived in the West just as the Rebels' position in southern Kentucky was disintegrating. The general was bitter at this state of affairs. "I am taking the helm when the ship of state is already on the breakers," he wrote to a friend in Congress. (Albert Sidney Johnston was still in command, but Beauregard described himself as "taking the helm.") After the Southerners abandoned the Kentucky line, they concentrated at Corinth, where Beauregard became second in command to Johnston. When Johnston died at Shiloh, Beauregard assumed command of the army.

Although the Rebels won considerable success on the first day at Shiloh, the arrival of Yankee reinforcements nullified their gains and forced Beauregard to draw his army back to Corinth.

The Federals followed slowly, and in late May Beauregard abandoned the town, withdrawing the Army of Tennessee to Tupelo, some fifty miles to the south. Beauregard was then in bad health, and in mid-June he left the army to spend a few days recuperating at Bladon Springs, near Mobile. President Davis quickly removed Beauregard from command of the army—ostensibly because the general had gone on sick leave without first obtaining proper authority from the government. In reality, Beauregard lost the command because Davis had neither affection for him nor confidence in his abilities.

Connelly observes that, by the time he came to the West, Beauregard was "steadily becoming an important member of a combined civilian-military anti-administration bloc." Beauregard, who wanted to command the Confederate army in Virginia and was frustrated and angered when the presence of a higher-ranking officer prevented his doing so, came west wanting to take command of the Army of Tennessee. "Evidently. . . [he] partially considered the West as a place of exile, a field where he would show Richmond that he had been misjudged," writes Connelly. He "also envisioned himself as the savior of the entire . . . [western Confederacy]." "He evidently believed he would be the real leader behind the scenes." His condescending "treatment of Johnston showed his desire to take over the Army of Tennessee." "Adept" at stirring up trouble, Beauregard was "somewhat vain." He became "totally discouraged" in April and May of 1862, and by that time he was "an avowed member of the anti-Davis faction in the Army and Congress." After being removed from command of the Army of Tennessee, Beauregard "spent the rest of the summer [of 1862] in Alabama fanning any available flames of resentment against Davis."

Although he was in some respects "a fine officer," Beauregard harbored a great hatred for Davis. The bitterness existing between himself and the government as well as the general's propensity to make what his biographer called "plans . . . not based on realities, and sometimes . . . almost fantastic" would have constituted most formidable obstacles to his success as commander of the Army of Tennessee. Any general whose favorite plans "grated against government strategic policy," as did many of Beauregard's, could not have worked well with a commander in chief like Davis.

One may well doubt if a general such as Beauregard could have successfully exercised command in the West even if he had been able to get along with Davis. Beauregard's "greatest weakness as a soldier," his biographer T. Harry Williams admitted, was his tendency "to think of war as something that was in books and that was fought in conformity to a fixed pattern. He could not easily adjust his thinking to an actual situation or improvise new ways of war. Too many times he would go by the rules in the book." Such an attitude on the part of a Rebel commander in the West would quickly have led him to disaster.[3]

As Beauregard's replacement, Davis selected General Braxton Bragg, a forty-five-year-old native of North Carolina, who was a member of the West Point Class of 1837. Bragg had served in the old army until 1856, when he resigned and became a planter in Louisiana. In his two decades of service in the United States Army he had won both a high reputation as an artillery officer and a widespread notoriety for contentiousness. There was a story in the army—valid, if not literally true—concerning what once happened when Bragg was stationed at a post where he was a company commander and was also acting as the post quartermaster. One day, in his capacity as company commander, he made out a requisition for some supplies for his company and sent it to the post quartermaster. Later, in the quartermaster's office, Bragg disapproved the request and returned it to the company. Then, acting again as company commander, he resubmitted the requisition accompanied by a long justification explaining why the supplies were necessary. As quartermaster, he then composed an equally long explanation as to why the request should be denied. Finally, unable to resolve the squabble between the company commander and the post quartermaster, Bragg referred the mass of correspondence to the post commander. That worthy is supposed to have read the file and then to have exclaimed, "My god, Captain Bragg! You have quarrelled with everybody in the Army, and now you are quarrelling with yourself!"

In 1861 Bragg entered the military service of Louisiana, but he soon received an appointment as a general officer in the Confederate army. He spent the first year of the war on the Gulf Coast, where his primary responsibilities were to train troops and to defend Pensacola and Mobile. In the spring of 1862 he, along with most of his Gulf Coast troops, joined the Army of Tennessee at Corinth. He commanded a corps of the army at Shiloh.

After taking command of the army, Bragg launched it on one of the great offensive campaigns of the war. Using the western railroads, he swung his army around from Tupelo through Mobile to Chattanooga. Once transferred to southeastern Tennessee, Bragg's army, acting in loose concert with troops from Virginia and East Tennessee, marched northward into Kentucky. The Confederates hoped that the Bluegrass State would rise up and expel its Yankee occupiers and that thousands of its young men would flock to enroll in the Rebel ranks.

Most Kentuckians, however, refused to join or even to support the Confederates, and after an indecisive fight with the Federals at Perryville on 8 October, Bragg fell back into Tennessee. At Murfreesboro, Tennessee, on 31 December 1862 and 2 January 1863, he fought another battle. Again, the results on the field were not decisive, but again Bragg fell back.

In the late summer of 1863 Bragg was maneuvered out of his position around Tullahoma, Tennessee, and fell back into North Georgia, losing the important city of Chattanooga in the process. The Confederate government, alarmed at the danger to the central South, sent Lieutenant General James Longstreet with two divisions from Virginia to reinforce Bragg. More troops were sent from other points.

With the help of his reinforcements, Bragg turned on the Northerners at Chickamauga in North Georgia and defeated them on 19–20 September. The Yankees fled back to Chattanooga, and Bragg followed. The Confederates took up a position on the heights south and east of the town and waited for the Yankees to withdraw. While Bragg waited, the Yankee government rushed reinforcements to help the beleaguered garrison at Chattanooga. In late November, the Federals attacked Bragg's army and chased it south to Dalton, Georgia. Disgraced and under heavy criticism, Bragg resigned from command of the Army of Tennessee.

Most historians have not held a high opinion of Bragg, and certainly the general had his problems. T. Harry Williams called him "probably the ugliest and most disliked Southern general." According to Connelly, Bragg "never learned how to communicate with anyone." He had "suffered for years from a collection of ailments ranging from dyspepsia to severe migraine headaches. These had colored his personality, and . . . he had a dullness and sourness which often made him quarrelsome." In appearance he was "stooped, thin, and haggard." "With a mind too moody to dare and too administrative to deliver a lightning blow, Bragg was a brave soldier and a good provider—but he was not a fighter." Under pressure, "he would become pensive and fretful, would sulk [and] lose his sense of balance." Often he "lost his nerve" or "panicked." He was handicapped by "his constant fear of making a mistake and his consequent hesitation in committing his troops." He did not understand the value of terrain. He "always looked for infringements on his prerogatives by his superiors and for infractions of rules by his subordinates."

Bragg was "dull, sour, pedantic," and "did not seem to understand people." "He sought scapegoats for every mistake," and there were many mistakes for which scapegoats had to be found. "He never admitted a fault, except to say that he had entrusted [his subordinate] generals with tasks they were not good enough to perform." Often he "publicly humiliated his generals by arrest, damnation in reports to Richmond, and by other devices." Not surprisingly, he quarreled continuously with many of his generals, and the quarrels consumed both his time and his psychic energies. Bragg "became easily upset when obstacles seemed to jeopardize his plans, and he tended to magnify problems out of proportion." Battered by criticism and "as rigid as he was indecisive," Bragg, by late 1863, "was suffering from the beginnings of a nervous and physical breakdown."[4]

If President Davis had in the Rebel military hierarchy a more bitter enemy than Beauregard, it was General Joseph E. Johnston. Born in Virginia in 1807, Johnston had been graduated from West Point in 1829. He had served with distinction in the Seminole and Mexican wars and was quartermaster general of the United States Army when he resigned in 1861 to "go South." Appointed a general in the Rebel army, Johnston had commanded the Southern forces in Virginia until he was severely wounded in May 1862. When he was ready to return to duty the following November, Johnston was sent west and given vague powers over the Confederate armies in Tennessee and Mississippi. For the reasons discussed in Chapter 4, he was not successful in that post. By late 1863 his authority was limited to command of the woebegone Rebel forces in Mississippi.

Meanwhile, Johnston had had a monumental falling out with President Davis. The origins of their differences are not known. Some accounts trace the bitterness to their days at West Point (Davis was a member of the Class of 1828), when they are said to have been rivals for the attentions of a local damsel. Some authorities believe that the differences stemmed from the late antebellum years, when Davis, who was then chairman of the Senate Military Affairs Committee, is reported to have tried unsuccessfully to block Johnston's appointment as quartermaster general.

Whatever the ultimate origins of the estrangement, Davis's late summer 1861 decision regarding relative rank among Confederate generals brought the differences into the open. Confederate law provided that officers who left the United States Army and joined the Confederacy would hold the same relative rank that they had held in the old army. Johnston believed that his position as quartermaster general, which carried with it the "staff rank" of brigadier general, entitled him to the position as senior officer among all Rebel generals. Davis, however, decided to place Johnston based on his "permanent rank" of lieutenant colonel. The result was to put Johnston in fourth place on the list of Confederate generals. Johnston, a proud, touchy man, resented what he regarded as an unfair insult. The resulting dispute, often intemperate on both sides, "rankled through the whole history of the Confederacy" (to use the language of Johnston's biographers).

More disagreements over army organization, strategy, the failure to keep secrets, the assignment of officers, and other matters exacerbated the differences and widened the gulf between the two men. Johnston, like Beauregard, was very friendly with several members of Congress who were harsh critics of the president. Davis and the War Department bureaucrats sometimes sought to make Johnston the scapegoat for failures of Rebel strategy. Johnston himself sometimes committed serious strategic blunders.

By late 1863 Davis doubtless hoped that he could keep Johnston floundering around in the Mississippi swamps until the war was over. Johnston by then believed that the president was seeking to humiliate him by bringing about his defeat on the battlefield. Consequently, he viewed with a suspicion bordering on paranoia every action by the Richmond authorities that affected either him or his army. Johnston's well-known close connections with anti-Davis politicians and his carping, "often sarcastic, pedantic, and sometimes even childish letters" angered the president and other officials.

Johnston was very popular despite his faults, and he had a large following throughout both the military and civilian populations of the Confederacy. Consequently, in December 1863, after Bragg's manifest failure as commander, a great popular clamor arose to have Johnston take command of the Army of Tennessee. After trying unsuccessfully to find some other resolution for the problem of western command, Davis, at last and with great reluctance, yielded. In late December 1863, Johnston arrived in Dalton, Georgia, and the Army of Tennessee passed into his hands.

The six-and-a-half-month period of Johnston's tenure of command has stirred much controversy. During the winter months, Johnston reorganized the army and restored its morale. He and the government failed utterly, however, to work out a plan for the next campaign, and the Federal invasion of Georgia that began in May 1864 found the Rebels divided, uncertain of what they were trying to do, unable or unwilling to communicate with each other, and haggling over many matters. Johnston refused to divulge to the government any plan that he may have had and shrilly demanded that the authorities send him reinforcements. The government meddled in the internal affairs of the army and made unrealistic plans to have Johnston launch an invasion of East or Middle Tennessee. Most of these plans were made without consultation with Johnston.

Throughout May, June, and early July, Johnston fell back toward the crucial railroad and manufacturing center of Atlanta. With the general obviously unable or unwilling to devise any plan to halt the Yankee invasion of the keystone state of the Confederacy, Davis decided that a change of commanders was imperative. On 17 July he removed Johnston from command of the army. By that time the Rebels had been pushed back almost to the outskirts of Atlanta.

Johnston, Connelly writes with amazing understatement, "was no genius at strategy." He "exhibited a general air of defeatism." He was "a troubled man who seemed bitter and despondent" and was "not communicative." He "gave the impression that nothing pleased him and that whatever future arrangement was made probably would not please him either." He had "a relatively limited capacity as an overall commander." He "did not seem to grasp the picture of total war developing in Georgia in 1864." He possessed only a "limited comprehension of the campaign" that he waged for Atlanta, and he did not understand the political, economic, psychological, or diplomatic importance of the city. When he retreated to Atlanta in the summer of 1864, he abandoned virtually all of North Georgia and left completely exposed to the Yankees the great Confederate munitions complex around Selma, Alabama. Even Douglas Southall Freeman, who was very reluctant to write anything unfavorable about any Confederate officer, called Johnston "the most uncommunicative of all the senior officers with whom the President and the Secretary of War had to deal." In early 1865, when there was talk of putting him back in command, Johnston wrote that his relations with Davis were so bad that "no friend of mine or the country ought to wish to see me restored to command."[5]

Once Davis had determined to relieve Johnston from command, he had to choose his replacement. The president decided on young John Bell Hood, who had been born in Kentucky in 1831 and graduated from the Military Academy in 1853. Hood's rise to prominence had been meteoric. A lieutenant when he left the United States Army in the spring of 1861, Hood was soon made a colonel in the Rebel service and assigned to command the Fourth Texas Infantry Regiment. By the spring of 1862 he was a brigadier general. His brilliant combat leadership in several battles that summer won for him a well-deserved promotion to major general. In July 1863, at Gettysburg, he was severely wounded and lost the use of his left arm. Two months later, at Chickamauga, where his charging column broke through a gap in the Federal line, he was again wounded. His right leg was amputated just below the hip. Hood's leadership at Chickamauga won for him promotion to lieutenant general and assignment to command a corps in the Army of Tennessee. He functioned in that capacity until 17 July 1864, when he was named to succeed Johnston.

Soon after he took command of the Army, Hood struck at the Yankees around Atlanta. On 20, 22, and 28 July he lashed out at the Northerners about the city, trying to catch them off guard, destroy an isolated portion of their army, and force the remainder to retreat. Although Hood's attacks slowed the Federals' progress, he could not bring their advance to a halt. In early September the Yankees cut the last railroad that supplied Atlanta, and Hood was forced to abandon the city.

After he withdrew from Atlanta, Hood led the Army of Tennessee off on what was probably the most poorly planned and executed major campaign of the war. The Rebels swung west-ward into northwestern Alabama, where, after long delays, they got across the Tennessee River and marched northward toward Nashville. At Spring Hill on 29 November, Hood and his gener-als fumbled away an opportunity to strike a serious blow at the enemy, and on the following day an angry, frustrated, and disap-pointed Hood sent the army into a suicidal assault on a strong Yankee position at Franklin. Although the Federals withdrew after the battle, Hood's attack at Franklin was a failure and cost him more than six thousand men.

Unable to think of a better plan, Hood, on 1 December, followed the retreating Yankees northward to Nashville. There he took up a line on the hills south of the city and waited, hoping for reinforcements. While Hood waited, the Federals built up their strength. On 15 and 16 December they sallied out from the city, smashed into Hood's army, routed it, and sent the Rebels fleeing southward. Hood was lucky to have any organized force left by the time he got to Corinth, Mississippi, the army's birth-place. In late January 1865, Hood left the army, turning it over to Lieutenant General Richard Taylor.

In Connelly's opinion, Hood was even worse than Joseph E. Johnston. Hood was an ambitious troublemaker who had suf-fered two crippling wounds. He was also in love with and en-gaged to the beautiful Sally Buchanan Campbell Preston, and his burning ambition "may have been caused by the urgency to prove himself a man" despite his wounds. He was, writes Connelly, "a simple man, often tactless and crude, more of a fighter than a general." He was also "a chronic liar." In late July 1864, when he took command of the army, Hood was "a troubled man," be-deviled by "an intense and driving ambition to save Atlanta and to maintain his image as a hero." "Almost to the point of being psychotic," writes Connelly, Hood "associated valor with casualty figures."[6]

Never again after the Battle of Nashville did the Army of Tennessee fight as an army. Some of its units reached North Carolina in time to join Joseph E. Johnston for the final battles there. Others were sent to Mobile, where some of them literally ended the war in the waters of Mobile Bay, fighting to save that city. Still other units were strung out along the roads from Mississippi to North Carolina when the end finally came in the spring of 1865.

It was the misfortune of the Rebels' western army to have been burdened with a set of incompetent leaders from Gideon Pillow at the start of the war to Joseph E. Johnston at its end. It was suggested in Chapter 3 that only a computer could determine whether a Federal army under Grant, Sherman, Thomas, and Sheridan could have defeated a Rebel force under Lee, Longstreet, Jackson, and Stuart. Some historian who really wants to melt the microchips might try asking one of the infernal machines what would have happened if a Union army led by McClellan, Pope, Burnside, and Hooker had tangled with a band of Rebels under Joseph E. Johnston, Bragg, Hood, and Pillow.

WHILE the Johnstons, Beauregard, Bragg, and Hood were passing through the revolving door that was the command structure of the Army of Tennessee—"the comedy of Confederate Western command," the historian Emory M. Thomas calls it— and while that army's interminable internecine quarrels were destroying its generals, the Army of Northern Virginia achieved and maintained a high degree of command stability under the leadership of General Robert E. Lee. Lee was the offspring of a distinguished Virginia family. His father had been a general in the War for Independence and a governor of the state. Lee had been born in 1807 and had been graduated from West Point standing second in the Class of 1829 (Joseph E. Johnston had been thirteenth). Lee's record in the United States Army had been especially distinguished. In the spring of 1861 he had declined an offer to command the Federal army and had returned to Virginia.

After serving as commander of the state forces of the Old Dominion, Lee was appointed a general in the Confederate army. He briefly held commands in western Virginia and along the South Atlantic Coast until March 1862, when he returned to Richmond to serve as the military adviser to the president. On 1 June 1862, following Joseph E. Johnston's wounding, Davis named Lee to command the Army of Northern Virginia. Lee held the post for the remainder of that army's existence.

At the time Lee was appointed to command the Virginia army, it was backed up to the Rebel capital, and the outlook for the Southern cause was bleak. Within three months, Lee had driven one Yankee army away from the capital, defeated another in northern Virginia and chased it into the fortifications of Washington, and was preparing to advance across the Potomac River and carry the war into the North. At Fredericksburg in December 1862 and at Chancellorsville in May 1863, Lee won crushing victories. In the summer of 1863 he launched a second invasion of the North, and in 1864 and 1865 he skillfully directed a long and stubborn defense of Virginia against a massive Federal invasion.

The victories that Lee won were in part the results of all the political, economic, geographical, psychological, and military advantages enjoyed by the Rebel army in Virginia. In part, too, they resulted from Lee's many hours of labor over the administration of his army. For example, he constantly tinkered with its organization, seeking to make it more responsive to his orders.

Perhaps nothing better illustrates Lee's ability as an army administrator than the way he dealt with general officers who did not measure up to his standards. Skilled in the ways of military bureaucracy, Lee was able tactfully to secure the transfer of such officers. During his first great campaign, the Seven Days' Battle in June and July 1862, Lee discovered that some of his generals did not perform well, and he could discern nothing in their records to indicate that they were likely to improve. Without fuss or fanfare, these officers were transferred to other assignments. The flamboyant Major General John B. ("Prince John") Magruder wound up commanding the District of Texas, New Mexico, and Arizona. Major General Benjamin Huger was quietly relieved of command and assigned to duty as an inspector of artillery and ordnance. Eventually he was sent to the Trans-Mississippi Department. Major General Theophilus H. Holmes was sent to command the Trans-Mississippi Department. A few months later Lee quietly engineered the transfer of Brigadier General W. H. C. Whiting to open up a slot for the promotion of John Bell Hood.

Lee did not engage in personal quarrels with his generals, and when arguments broke out between his subordinates, the commanding general worked assiduously to resolve or restrain them and to limit the damage they did to the army. The best-known example of Lee's role as a conciliator was his 1862–63 effort to mitigate the simmering dispute between Stonewall Jackson and A. P. Hill.[7]

Lee's aloofness from, and his patient work in trying to resolve the disputes between, his generals was in marked contrast to the sad state of affairs in the Army of Tennessee—especially during the long, unhappy period when Braxton Bragg led the western army. Bragg became embroiled in bitter personal controversies with some of his generals that he was unable to resolve. As a result, quarrels among the generals of the Army of Tennessee tended to place many officers in opposition to the commanding general and to fester on and on, becoming more bitter with each passing week.

In the summer of 1862, for example, Bragg had a falling out with his two corps commanders, Leonidas Polk and William J. Hardee. The dispute seems to have grown from Bragg's well-founded belief that Polk was not fully competent as a corps commander. Bragg was especially disappointed at Polk's poor generalship during the Kentucky Campaign of 1862 and angered both by Polk's attempt to cast him in a bad light and by Polk's propensity to ignore military channels and deal directly with the government. Bragg's other corps commander, Hardee, became disgusted with Bragg and allied himself with Polk. Throughout late 1862 and until the fall of 1863, one or both of the corps commanders of the Army of Tennessee, in effect, led a clique of generals in opposition to the army's commander. They were opposed by another, smaller band of generals who were loyal to Bragg.

The civil war within the Army of Tennessee came to a head in the fall of 1863. In the previous July Hardee had been transferred to Mississippi, and in late September Bragg determined to purge the army of his other enemies. Bragg, however, soon found himself battling not only Polk but also Lieutenant General Daniel Harvey Hill, who had replaced Hardee, and Longstreet, who had brought reinforcements from Virginia and who probably coveted command of the western army for himself.

So bad did the situation become that, in early October, twelve generals signed a petition asking that Bragg be removed from command of the army. Several others doubtless would have signed, but they had been placed under arrest by Bragg and sent away from the army. Still others, known enemies of Bragg, refused to sign, perhaps because they feared reprisals. One general, Nathan Bedford Forrest, threatened to kill Bragg and announced that he would no longer obey orders from army headquarters. Even enlisted men were aware of the feuding among their leaders. One of them wrote, "I am sorry to say there is a great want of harmony among our generals at present. . . . All are down on Bragg; want him removed."

Alarmed at the uproar in the West, President Davis paid a visit to the Army of Tennessee. At a meeting on 9 October, Davis, with an embarrassed Bragg present, listened as, one after another, the leaders of the army condemned their general and asked that he be removed from command. Davis, who had probably made up his mind sometime before the meeting began, decided to sustain Bragg even though that general clearly did not have the confidence of his chief subordinates.

Supported by the president, Bragg resumed his campaign to punish his enemies in the army. One by one they were sent off to other areas or their commands were reorganized to deprive them of support. Brigades commanded by anti-Bragg brigadiers were transferred to divisions led by Bragg's friends or by officers who were neutral; brigades commanded by Bragg's supporters were put into divisions led by his enemies among the major generals. Bragg hoped thus to disperse and neutralize his critics. He even jumped at the chance to rid himself of Longstreet by sending that general and his two divisions off to operate against Knoxville.

As a result of all these changes, Bragg, by mid-November 1863, had triumphed over his enemies in the Army of Tennessee and sent away or otherwise humiliated his critics among the generals. He had also demoralized his troops by separating them from the generals who had led them throughout the war and from other units with which they had served through many a bloody fight. Finally, he had fatally weakened the army by sending Longstreet off into East Tennessee. When the Federals struck at him in late November, his army collapsed.

Bragg's departure from command did not end the discord among the high-ranking western generals, although never again did it reach such titanic proportions. In the 1864 Georgia Campaign, for example, Hardee, who had returned to the army to lead a corps, seems to have resented Joseph E. Johnston's "cavalier attitude" toward him and to have been irritated by Johnston's tendency to make decisions without sufficient consultation with the senior corps commander. Hardee also resented Hood's July promotion to full general (Hardee outranked Hood as lieutenant general), and he did not give Hood his complete support and cooperation. Hardee left the army after the fall of Atlanta.[8]

Another major difference between Lee and his western counterparts was that the Virginia commander wisely refrained from becoming involved with the anti-Davis politicians. Joseph E. Johnston and Beauregard were openly identified with the critics of the administration, and they sometimes furnished their congressional friends with information that was embarrassing to the president. Critics of the chief executive, wrote Richard Taylor, "gathered themselves behind [Joseph E. Johnston's] . . . shield and shot arrows at President Davis." When Beauregard could not obtain approval from the War Department for one of his proposals, he often wrote members of Congress or other political figures expressing dissatisfaction with Davis and his advisers.

Finally, he exploded to Representative William Porcher Miles about Davis: "The curse of God must have been on our people when we chose him [as president]."[9]

Davis considered himself an expert in military matters, and he liked to involve himself in the details of army administration. Perhaps he was psychologically reverting to his days as secretary of war in the United States government (1853–57). Throughout the time that he commanded the Army of Northern Virginia, Lee was always careful to communicate with the government, to consult with the president and the secretary of war about matters that affected his army, and to comply with the wishes and orders of the civilian authorities.

Lee's correspondence is full of letters and telegrams to the government dealing with logistics, plans, and the organization of his army. On 20 May 1863, for example, Lee wrote a long letter to Davis, expressing concern for the president's health and discussing the organization of the Army of Northern Virginia— down to which colonels should be promoted to brigadiers—and, with great deference, proposing that the army be divided into three (rather than two) corps. Lee discussed at length the reasons for the proposed restructuring of his command and the several officers who might be promoted to fill the vacancies created by the new organization. The letter is filled with courteous phrases: "I propose to submit to the consideration of Your Excellency"; "If therefore you think"; "I submit to your better judgment"; "I hope you will be able to give me your conclusions at your earliest convenience"; and "With earnest wishes for your health & happiness, & with great respect, I am your obt servt."[10]

One searches almost in vain for similar respectful letters from the western commanders. On 16 February 1864, for example, Joseph E. Johnston asked to have the Army of Tennessee divided into three corps. Johnston's short request was sent to Adjutant and Inspector General Samuel Cooper. His justification for the proposed change was contained in one curt sentence. The new organization, he wrote, would be more convenient, and it would permit easier handling and maneuvering of the army. Johnston requested that Major General Mansfield Lovell be sent to the army and made the commander of the new corps. Lovell was in disgrace for the 1862 loss of New Orleans, and—although Johnston might not have been aware of it—he was also rapidly becoming identified as an anti-Davis general. To make matters even worse, Johnston's request had been preceded by a letter written from Johnston's headquarters by Tennessee Governor Isham G. Harris to the secretary of war, who sent it on to Davis. Harris was very critical of the existing organization of the army, which, he wrote, "I understand . . . was required by an order of the President, which prevents General Johnston from interfering with it." (This was a reference to Bragg's late 1863 reorganization that was designed to scatter his enemies.) Not surprisingly, Johnston's proposal to form a third corps in the Army of Tennessee was disapproved on the grounds that the army was then too small to justify division into three corps.[11]

Lee knew that the Richmond authorities were naturally concerned about the progress of his campaigns, and he went to great lengths to keep them informed about the details of his army's movements, the enemy's activities in his front, and his plans. Such was not the case with the Army of Tennessee. Three times during the war Davis left Richmond and traveled to Tennessee and Georgia to visit the western army. In addition, he almost always had telegraphic contact with that army's commanding general. Despite the visits and telegrams, Davis and the Richmond authorities were often ignorant of the Army of Tennessee's location, its strength, its problems, the doings of the enemy in its front, and its commanders' plans.

Five men were responsible for this ignorance on the part of the government officials—Albert Sidney Johnston, P. G. T. Beauregard, Braxton Bragg, Joseph E. Johnston, and John Bell Hood. In the week of 22–28 May 1864, for example, Joseph E. Johnston sent only two brief messages to Richmond about the crucial campaign that he was then conducting in North Georgia. One of these messages went to Davis, the other to Bragg, who was then serving as the president's military adviser. During the same week,

Lee wrote four letters to Davis, dispatched six telegrams to the secretary of war, and, for good measure, sent a telegram to Bragg.[12]

The commanding generals of the Army of Tennessee simply did not provide the Rebel government with information about their army and what it was doing. Indeed, in some cases, as with Braxton Bragg, when he was maneuvered out of Tullahoma and Chattanooga in 1863, and Joseph E. Johnston's loss of Dalton, Georgia, in 1864, it is certain that the commanders of the western army did not know what was happening in their front.

SOUND administration and close cooperation with the government helped to make Lee's army better than its western counterpart, but by themselves they do not explain the success it enjoyed. The explanation for most of the eastern army's success is to be found in Lee himself, mostly in his intelligence and his character. Lee could learn from his experiences. He could devise bold, daring plans. Lee had the intelligence and the moral courage to put his plans into execution, and he would accept the responsibility if they failed. He stands as the colossus of Confederate military history—the only Southern army commander to enjoy any degree of success.

A Virginian who served with both the Army of Northern Virginia and the Army of Tennessee best summed it up. The basic difference between the two great Rebel armies, he declared, "is that one of them has Gen'l Lee and the other—has'nt."[13]

CHAPTER NINE

Historians and Generals

T his book had its origins in a paper I prepared for the May 1983 meeting of the Confederate Historical Institute in Murfreesboro, Tennessee. That paper, which bore the title "The Army of Tennessee versus the Army of Northern Virginia," contained in abridged form the theses set forth in Chapters 5 through 8 of this work. That paper, like this essay, was to a great degree a collection of ideas about and a response to a debate that has flared up from time to time since 1969 between Professor Thomas L. Connelly and some of his allies on one side and Professor Albert Castel on the other. It seems, therefore, appropriate to summarize that debate before closing with my own thoughts on the subject.[1]

The central figure in the debate was Robert E. Lee. For decades Lee had been so praised by most writers on the war that it was very difficult to get a realistic understanding of his character and personality. Many almost idolatrous biographers had portrayed him as a man virtually without personal flaws and as a general who never made a mistake. In 1969 Connelly launched an effort both to reexamine Lee as a person and to reevaluate his role in the Civil War. In "Robert E. Lee and the Western Confederacy: A Criticism of Lee's Strategic Ability," Connelly sallied forth both to protest what he called "the colonial status of the western Confederate army in . . . Civil War writing and thinking" and to take a new look at Lee's personality, his record as an army commander, and his role as a Civil War strategist. Connelly wanted to "depict . . . Lee as he actually was."

Arguing that Lee "seems to have benefited from special pleading" and that "a balanced treatment of his personality may have been lost in the aura and glamor of the Virginia segment of the war," Connelly took Lee to task on "three major counts, personality, field success, and strategy." For Lee, wrote Connelly, "personality faults have become virtues. His weakness in handling subordinate officers, his seemingly submissive approach in dealing with Jefferson Davis, and his disinterest in political matters have been praised as evidence of his great kindness, his respect, and his sole interest in the military." By using such faulty criteria, Connelly suggested, earlier writers had "perhaps shaped . . . [Lee] into a semi-religious symbol of suffering and resignation for a disillusioned, distraught [post-1865] South."

Connelly then proceeded to an attack on Lee's military reputation. He criticized the Virginian's "penchant for the offensive," which, he wrote, resulted in far higher casualties than the Confederacy could afford. Connelly also wondered whether Lee's success would have been as great or his reputation as high if he had had to face such skillful generals as the Federals had in the West, to deal with the problems of geography and logistics that faced the leaders of the Army of Tennessee, to work within a command structure similar to that of the western army, and to face the heavy numerical advantage, which, he claimed, the western Yankees enjoyed. Connelly, for example, pointed out that Lee's campaigns in the East were conducted in an area of only 22,000 square miles whereas the Army of Tennessee campaigned over a region embracing 225,000 square miles and stretching across seven states, where there were few railroads and the river systems offered to the Federals "excellent avenues of penetration deep into the West."

The bulk of Connelly's article, however, was devoted to a criticism of Lee as a grand strategist. Before assuming command of the Army of Northern Virginia, Lee had served as a military adviser to President Davis. That assignment was never formally terminated, and, Connelly maintained, Lee continued to advise the government on military matters in all areas of the Confederacy throughout the war. Lee was, in fact, about the only individual military leader to carry much weight with the president. Unfortunately for the Rebels, "Lee possessed an almost startling lack of knowledge of the West"; he was uninformed about Federal strength and Confederate weakness in the area; he did not understand western geography or grasp fully the importance of the munitions-producing area of Georgia, Tennessee, and Alabama; and he underestimated the logistical problems of maneuver in the West. Lee believed that the main war zone was in Virginia, and that conviction plus his ignorance of the situation in the West led him frequently to propose that the Army of Tennessee be stripped of troops to reinforce his own army in Virginia.

Lee's "obsession with Virginia" shaped his ideas about strategy. "One might also debate," Connelly wrote, "whether Lee possessed a sufficiently broad military mind to deal with overall Confederate matters. . . . Lee seemed to evince a more localistic provincial outlook than did other major Confederate leaders, so much so that one might perhaps infer that Lee was fighting for Virginia and not for the South." He saw Confederate strategy as "essentially the salvation of Virginia."[2]

This assault on Lee did not long go unanswered. In 1970 Albert Castel sprang to Lee's defense with a counterblast entitled "The Historian and the General: Thomas L. Connelly versus Robert E. Lee." Branding Connelly's article "pseudo-history" full of "errors and distortions" and his criticisms of Lee "either unfounded, excessive, or pointless," Castel waded into an item-by-item refutation of Connelly's arguments. He pointed out that Lee's reputation as a man of unusually high character had been the subject of prewar comments and therefore could not have been the product of a postdefeat search for a semireligious symbol. Although Lee suffered heavy casualties, Castel asserted, he did win victories—despite the fact that his army was outnumbered in every major battle it fought. On many occasions, Castel pointed out, the Army of Tennessee outnumbered, or was approximately equal to, its opponent, and yet it almost always lost. The Army of Northern Virginia inflicted heavier casualties on the Yankees than did the Army of Tennessee. Moreover, Castel pointed out, Lee protected the important city of Richmond, and, if he put great emphasis on the war in Virginia, so did many others. Finally, Castel asserted, the Army of Tennessee lost its battles because its generals were incompetent, not because of anything that Lee or the Confederate government did.[3]

In 1973 Connelly, reinforced by Archer Jones, again took out after the greatest Rebel of them all. The two historians included a chapter entitled "Robert E. Lee and Confederate Strategy" in their fine book *The Politics of Command: Factions and Ideas in Confederate Strategy*. In that chapter they reiterated Connelly's earlier argument that Lee was, throughout the war, in a position to exercise a great influence on the overall Rebel war effort. In that role, Lee focused his attention almost exclusively on the Yankee threat to Virginia, and his basic idea of overall strategy was that other Southern armies should either send some—or all—of their troops to reinforce the Confederate army in Virginia or attack the Yankees in their front so as to compel the Federals to reduce their forces in Virginia in order to strengthen the points at which they were being assailed by the other Rebels. Connelly and Jones repeated the former's earlier arguments that Lee neither understood the geographical and military conditions in the West nor appreciated the region's importance to the Confederacy. "Lee's interest in the West," they assert, "seemed limited to what the region could do to help Virginia."[4]

In the same year that his collaborative effort with Jones appeared, Connelly also published "The Image and the General: Robert E. Lee in American Historiography." In this article, Connelly explained some of his ideas about the "process by which . . . [Lee's] image has developed in American letters since the Civil War." Virginia authors and interest in Virginia affairs, Connelly argued, have given those who are attracted to the war in the Old Dominion "control of both Confederate historiography and of most memorial and veterans organizations." This control, Connelly believes, has "provided Lee with a base of publicity enjoyed by no other prominent former Confederate." Connelly also suggested that Lee's image has been enhanced because he "provided certain needed symbolism for both the southern and the national minds." Late nineteenth-century Southern whites—the

Confederate generation—used Lee as a "Christ-symbol" for their lost cause. The great Virginian was a chivalrous man whose spotless life proved that the just, virtuous, heroic individual did not always enjoy worldly success. Sometimes God's larger purpose was served when such a man experienced defeat in the largely meaningless contests of this world. After 1900, Connelly maintained, Lee became a national "hero symbol" whose abhorrence of slavery, devotion to duty, and postwar effort to lead the Southern people back into the Union were fitting models for all Americans. The real Lee, Connelly argued, was lost in the mythology that enveloped Lee the symbol.[5]

Four years later Connelly returned to the assault with the publication of *The Marble Man: Robert E. Lee and His Image in American Society*. The book is, in fact, two different works published under one cover. The longer and better work is an exercise in social-literary-intellectual history in which Connelly traces the image of Lee through both Southern and American literature from the wartime writings in which he shared glory with several other Rebel heroes to the great biography by Douglas Southall Freeman (1934–35), by which time the general had become the "central figure" of Southern history. The first part of *The Marble Man* is a fascinating attempt to explain the way Lee came to be depicted—and deified—in Southern writing. It is, in fact, an elaboration of Connelly's 1973 article.

The shorter part of *The Marble Man* is more relevant to this essay. It is a fifty-seven-page epilogue in which Connelly attempts to probe "beneath the protective coating of the Lee image" to find a "personality [that] has been obscured by a century of near sainthood" and by so doing to make visible the "inner Lee."

Once Connelly removed the "protective coating," he found what he believed to have been the "real Lee." That man was "not the simple character portrayed by many authors" but a complex individual marked by "savage outbursts of temper," "deep moods of depression," a "long-time fixation with death," as well as "elements of frustration, self-doubt, and unhappiness."

All of these traits, Connelly hypothesized, had their origins in Lee's "abnormal boyhood experience," when family circumstances forced him to spend his time caring for his mother; in his haunting fear that he would disgrace the family as his father and half-brother had done by being imprisoned for debt, losing a fortune in speculation, and carrying on an affair with a relative's wife; in his marriage—"a near formality"—that "did not provide him with the emotional satisfaction he desired"; in his "sense of failure" as an officer in the antebellum army in which promotions came slowly; and in his sense of personal sin and unworthiness, which led him to a "moral estrangement from God."

Having thus established—at least to his own satisfaction—that he had found the real Lee and that this man was as wretched as the pathetic beings who people the pages of his books on the Army of Tennessee, Connelly proceeded to try to discern the way in which the burdens, strains, and frustrations that afflicted his unhappy subject influenced, if they did not determine, his conduct during the Civil War. Connelly believed that he had found the answer in psychological theories that link inner moods with "aggressiveness or warlike tendencies." Although Connelly admitted that the scholars whose ideas he cites "often disagree on . . . [the] nature" of the relationship between such moods and aggressive behavior, he uses their general concept as the framework on which to hang his theory that Lee's boldness and aggressive conduct of military operations stemmed at least in part from his "repressed personality." "War thus provided an emotional release for a man who had contained strong emotions beneath a mantle of reserve."

Finally, Connelly expressed the idea that Lee's antebellum conviction that he was a failure may have contributed to his wartime boldness. Like his Northern counterpart, Ulysses S. Grant, Lee saw himself in 1861 as a man who had never achieved success. Since neither he nor Grant had a reputation to uphold, neither man feared failure, and in both "there may have been an inherent willingness to act boldly in order to prove that they had the capacity for success."[6]

The latest round in the debate—so far—came in 1982, when Connelly and Barbara L. Bellows published *God and General Longstreet: The Lost Cause and the Southern Mind*. This work includes a chapter titled "Robert E. Lee and the Southern Mind" in which Connelly's earlier ideas about the general's "true personality" are again trotted out, this time as "an exaggeration" of the common traits of Southerners, "a paradox of extremes," and "the greatest paradox of a paradoxical South."[7]

In his several writings about Lee, Connelly expounds three different but related themes. One theme deals with the real Lee, who, Connelly believes, was a man troubled by inner doubts, frustrations, and convictions of his own unworthy nature. A second theme revolves around what Connelly believes to be the false interpretation of Lee that resulted from the hagiographical writings of his biographers. The third theme deals with Lee's role as a Civil War general and especially with his effort to concentrate Confederate military resources for the defense of Virginia. It is this last theme that is most directly relevant to this book, for Connelly believes that throughout the war Lee and Davis exhibited a "blindness to western problems."[8]

During most of the Civil War the Confederates carried on a continuing debate over the proper grand strategy that they should employ in their effort to win independence. In its most basic terms, this debate involved the question of whether the Rebels should concentrate the greater part of their scant resources in Virginia or in the West. On one side of the debate was Lee, who argued that Virginia was the most significant front and that, if necessary, it should be sustained by drawing upon other regions for men and matériel. On 3 September 1862, for example, as he was preparing for his first invasion of the North, Lee wrote President Davis suggesting that "should Genl Bragg find it impracticable to operate to advantage on his present frontier [in Tennessee and Kentucky], his army, after leaving sufficient garrisons, could be advantageously employed in opposing the overwhelming numbers which it seems to be the intention of the enemy now to concentrate in Virginia."[9]

The men on the other side of the debate were led by Beauregard. They opposed the Davis administration's policy of trying to defend all of the important points in the western Confederacy (a "cordon defense") and advocated instead that some western territory be temporarily given up to permit the concentration of Rebel manpower for an offensive strike against some important but weak point in the Federal position in the West. Like Halleck, these Confederate leaders wanted to adopt Jomini's idea of concentrating on some decisive point where the enemy was weak. The members of this "western concentration bloc" were also deeply concerned about the fate of the central South—the Nashville-Chattanooga-Atlanta corridor. The importance of the area, they believed, was not fully appreciated by Davis and Lee, who worried more about Virginia and the Mississippi Valley.

The western concentration bloc was made up of four subgroups (some of which had their own subfactions), and it included many men who were bitter personal enemies. Braxton Bragg on one hand and many of his most implacable critics such as John C. Breckinridge, Leonidas Polk, and William J. Hardee on the other could agree on little except the idea that a greater share of Rebel resources should be allocated to the West.

Given Lee's proximity to Richmond, his far more frequent communications with the government, his better personal compatibility with the president, and the great prestige that came from his impressive string of victories in Virginia, one would expect to find Davis eagerly accepting his advice to concentrate in the Old Dominion. Davis, for some reason, did no such thing. He never sent reinforcements directly from the Army of Tennessee to Lee, and rarely after the opening months of the war did he use any western troops to reinforce the Army of Northern Virginia. In fact, on several occasions the president took troops from Virginia and sent them west. In the winter of 1861–62 at least five units—three Tennessee regiments, an Alabama regiment, and a Georgia battalion—that had rushed to Virginia the preceding summer were sent to Tennessee. They were joined in the West by John B. Floyd's brigade, which had spent the early months of the war in western Virginia. In the summer of 1862 troops under Humphrey Marshall were sent from southwestern Virginia to cooperate with Bragg's army in its Kentucky Campaign. In the late summer of 1863 Longstreet took two of the finest divisions in Lee's army from Virginia to reinforce the Army of Tennessee in North Georgia. In the winter of 1864–65 Lee sent seven brigades from his army to the Carolinas to reinforce the remnants of the Army of Tennessee then fighting in that area.

Virginia was not the only source from which reinforcements were sent to the western Confederacy. In the spring of 1862 troops from the Trans-Mississippi crossed the great river and joined the Army of Tennessee at Corinth. A few weeks earlier, Davis virtually stripped the Gulf Coast from Florida to the Rio Grande to strengthen the Rebel forces concentrating at Corinth—and soon after doing so he lost Pensacola and New Orleans. In 1862 and again in 1863 Davis sent reinforcements west from the South Atlantic Coast in futile efforts to save Corinth and Vicksburg, and in early 1864 Brigadier General Hugh W. Mercer's brigade and some cavalry regiments were sent from Savannah to reinforce the Army of Tennessee. In 1863 and 1864 other troops were sent to the Army of Tennessee from the Mobile area.

Davis may have paid far more attention to the nearby military operations in Virginia, but he did not allow his preoccupation with the Old Dominion to result in a diversion of manpower from the West to the East.

As president, Davis listened to both sides in the debate between Lee and the western concentration bloc. The help that he occasionally sent to the West notwithstanding, Davis could never bring himself to make a clear decision between the two opposing concepts of Rebel strategy. The two sides of the debate were of about equal strength, and the president, caught between them, was paralyzed. Instead of developing an overall Rebel war plan and making a clear choice, Davis took the politician's easy way out—he tried to please both sides by dividing Confederate resources more or less equally between East and West. As a result, the Southerners attempted to operate in both Virginia and the West at levels they could not sustain.

Faced with the personal hostility toward himself of some of the western generals and their more or less open alliance with the congressional and journalistic critics of his administration, kept to a great degree uninformed of the situation in the West by both the ignorance and the reticence of many of his western commanders, and well aware of the indisputable fact that the western Rebel generals lost almost every battle they fought even when their army outnumbered its enemy, it is no wonder that Davis came to look upon the Virginia theater as the arena in which the South could win her independence. The wonder—and, in fact, the indication of his fairness to the West—is that Davis gave as much time and resources to that region as he did.

One of the themes that runs through much of the writing on the American Civil War is the idea that the Confederate government overcommitted itself to the Virginia theater. A concomitant theme that emerges in Connelly's attack on Lee is that the Virginian, although never able to win Davis over to his proposal for a concentration in the East, had enough influence to prevent a concentration in the West. Thus the western generals never had an army strong enough to implement their ideas for an offensive concentration against some weak point in the Federal position between the Appalachians and the Mississippi. Connelly's unspoken assumption is that such a strategy would have presented the Confederates with a better chance for victory than would either Lee's proposal to stage a massive concentration in Virginia and to fight the battle of annihilation there or Davis's practice of dividing Rebel resources about equally between East and West and not daring to make a choice between the two areas.[10]

Several comments seem to be in order.

First, Connelly's attacks on Lee for his personality and his battlefield successes are very weak. The matter of Lee's personality is irrelevant to the purposes of this essay and is a subject for Lee's biographers to debate with Connelly. It cannot be disputed that Lee enjoyed a great deal of success on the battlefield. Connelly, however, confuses cause and effect and ignores the extent to which Lee—unlike his western counterparts—was able, to a surprising degree, to shape the environment in which his army operated. Connelly wondered, for example, how Lee would have fared if he had had to work within a command structure similar to the wretched mess that existed in the high echelons of the Army of Tennessee. All of the evidence, as Castel pointed out in his reply to Connelly, indicates that Lee would have gone to work to change that messy arrangement, and, if his record in Virginia is any indication, he would have succeeded in doing so.

Connelly also makes much of the Army of Tennessee's handicap in operating over a vast area of almost a quarter of a million square miles in seven states while the eastern Rebel army campaigned in a compact area only one-tenth that size. What Connelly fails to note is that the Army of Tennessee operated over such a vast region because it could not hold any of its positions. When the Army of Tennessee went somewhere, it was usually because it was driven—if not chased—there by its enemy; when the Army of Northern Virginia went somewhere, it was usually because Lee ordered it to go there. In other words, the Army of Tennessee was not unsuccessful because it campaigned over a vast area; it campaigned over a vast area because it was unsuccessful.

Second, one must raise again some old questions about Jefferson Davis's role as commander in chief of the Confederate military and naval forces. It has long been a staple ingredient of professorial lectures that the Rebel chief executive wasted too much of his time and energy on military minutiae. What the Confederacy needed was some overall military plan, some central direction, for its war effort. Only the president could have formulated, won support for, and implemented such a plan. Except for his often ineffective scheme for temporary interdepartmental movements of troops for specific purposes, Davis failed utterly to provide such leadership.

Third, when Davis called upon Lee for overall advice after the general took command of the Army of Northern Virginia, the president put Lee in an impossible position. Every army commander faces at least two foes. One is the national enemy whom he meets on the battlefield; the other is the bureaucratic foe—the other parts of his own country's military establishment with which he competes for men and resources. Almost every commander believes that he holds the key position and that any reduction in his force will undermine the national security. Connelly criticizes Lee for his reluctance in 1863 to allow Longstreet to go west to reinforce the Army of Tennessee. Yet a few weeks after Longstreet arrived in the West, Bragg—motivated in large part by his antipathy for Longstreet—depleted the western army by detaching the two divisions under Longstreet's command and sending them off into the East Tennessee mountains. Soon afterward, Bragg's weakened army was routed at Missionary Ridge and fell back into Georgia. Longstreet's divisions, cut off from the Army of Tennessee, eventually returned to Virginia. Lee sent troops to the Army of Tennessee; Bragg sent them away. Perhaps there is something to be said for a general's holding on to his men.

Lee's advice to give primacy to the war in Virginia reflected both his own conviction that the Old Dominion was the most important theater of the conflict and the bureaucratic imperative that he preserve the strength of his own army. Connelly, of course, would maintain that Lee's belief in the supreme importance of the Old Dominion was based mostly on his Virginia provincialism and his ignorance of conditions in and the importance of the West.

Fourth, one must raise a basic question: Was Lee in error in believing that the Old Dominion was the most important part of the Confederacy? The data presented in Chapter 2 of this study give some indication of the state's importance to the Rebels. There can be little doubt that Virginia was far more important than any other Confederate state. Along with the Carolinas, she constituted the true economic heartland of the Southern nation—especially in the early stages of the war.

Fifth, the military conditions in the West were so favorable to the Yankees and so disadvantageous to the Confederates that one must wonder if any possible concentration of Rebel troops in the West would have produced a decisive victory there. To raise one obvious question, we might ask if Northern control of the Mississippi, Cumberland, and Tennessee rivers would have gone far to nullify the effects of any victory that the Southerners might have won in Mississippi, Alabama, or West and Middle Tennessee.

Sixth, given the gross, indeed, the almost criminal incompetence of the Confederate generals who served in the West—as those generals are described by Connelly himself—one must wonder if any possible number of reinforcements for their army would have made a difference. As Castel pointed out in his 1970 reply to Connelly, the Army of Northern Virginia never waged a major campaign in which its strength exceeded that of its enemy. The western Rebels, by contrast, outnumbered their opponents on the battlefield on six crucial occasions (the initial stages of the fighting around Fort Donelson, the prelude to and the first day at Shiloh, Pea Ridge, the early stages of the Vicksburg Campaign, Chickamauga, and Franklin). The results of these battles consisted of one barren, costly victory (Chickamauga) and five defeats—including two that ended with the surrender of Rebel armies (Fort Donelson and Vicksburg).

The conduct of the western Rebel generals during the Kentucky Campaign in the fall of 1862 was especially embarrassing for the Southerners. By itself, the history of that campaign should write *finis* to any lingering theory that overall Confederate military leadership was superior to that of the Federals. Early in the campaign, in September, the Confederates—thanks to hard marching—had gotten to Munfordville, where they were between the Union army and its supply base, astride the Yankees' railroad line of communications, and in a position where they could easily have concentrated a superior force to fight their enemy.

After throwing away that opportunity, the Confederate generals managed to get themselves so bamboozled and confused that they scattered their forces. As a result, at Perryville, on 16 October, sixteen thousand Confederates were thrown into a battle against thirty-six thousand Yankees. Helped by some bumbling on the part of the Union generals, by the fact that many of the Northern units were recently organized and hence inexperienced, and by their own superb courage, these sixteen thousand Rebels actually managed to win a tactical victory over their thirty-six thousand opponents—after which the Confederate generals decided to flee the state.

If Bragg had had, say, fifteen thousand more men at Chickamauga, would it have made a difference? Or would it only have meant that there were a few thousand more troops whose lives Bragg could waste and a few more generals in the Army of Tennessee with whom he could quarrel? Would Lee have wisely used fifteen thousand additional troops at Second Manassas? at Antietam? at Chancellorsville? at Mine Run?

Seventh, one must remember the basic strategy advocated by the western concentration bloc—find the weak points in the enemy's position in the West and concentrate for a quick offensive strike against them. As Jomini observed, the art of war "consisted precisely in recognizing these points." In view of their long, sorry record of petty bickering, missed opportunities, and general bungling, one must question whether the Rebel generals in the West could have found any Yankee weak points or managed to get themselves organized enough to strike a decisive blow against them even if they should somehow have managed to stumble across them.

Eighth, on the national level of grand strategy—the level at which Davis should have functioned for the South but did not—application of the western concentration bloc's basic idea would have led to the conclusion that the Yankees' weakest point was not in the West but in Virginia. Thus it would seem that Lee's advice (whatever its motive) was sound and that the Rebels should have concentrated in the Old Dominion to make there the supreme effort to achieve their independence. Conditions in Virginia were more favorable to the Southerners, and such a plan would have applied the western concentration bloc's basic strategy on a truly national level.

Ninth, if we accept Connelly's evaluations of the western Rebel generals, we are forced to admit that Lee was the only competent army commander the Confederacy had. Connelly calls him "the South's most successful field commander." He was, in fact, the South's only successful field commander and the only Rebel full general who could meet the criteria for a successful army commander discussed in Chapter 3 of this book. Even Connelly, while arguing that Lee was a troubled man, beset with frustration, doubt, disappointment, and unhappiness, admits that he was a great military leader. Much of his greatness, Connelly believes, "may have been due to his ability to control" the very disrupting elements of frustration and doubt which, Connelly argues, lurked just beneath the surface of his personality. Thus if we grant to Connelly every point that he argues about Lee's "real" personality, we, and he, are left with the patent fact that the great Virginian was the only Confederate army commander who ever demonstrated an ability to win victories on the battlefield. Unfortunately for the Southerners, Lee could not command both of the two great Rebel armies at the same time. Just as Lincoln was once reported to have requested that a barrel of Grant's whiskey be sent to each of the other Yankee generals, so Davis would have done well to find and send to the West another general with Lee's ability to rein in his personal problems, cooperate with the government and other Southern generals, inspire his troops, and win battles.

Finally, it seems that, as the Civil War evolved, the really decisive area—the theater where the outcome of the war was decided—was the West. The great Virginia battles and campaigns on which historians have lavished so much time and attention had, in fact, almost no influence on the outcome of the war. They led, at most, to a stalemate while the western armies fought the war of secession to an issue. This situation came about because Davis permitted overall strategic initiative to remain with the Federals, and they chose to accept a stalemate in Virginia and to concentrate their effort in the West.

Several historians have pointed out that the Confederacy could not have long survived without both Virginia and the West. The truth of the observation is self-evident. The Rebels' dilemma was that they did not have either the leadership or the manpower and matériel to hold both areas. Perhaps their only real chance for victory was to follow Lee's advice, trade space for time in the West—which is basically the way the war was fought there anyway—and concentrate their strength in Virginia and seek to gain their independence by an overwhelming victory over the Army of the Potomac and the capture of Washington, D.C.

Such a strategy would have employed their best army under their best general at the point where conditions were most favorable to them and where their enemy was at his weakest. If the Confederates could not have won their independence under such circumstances, they could not have won it anywhere under any possible conditions.[11]

Known Antebellum Military Experience of Confederate Generals

In the following list Confederate generals are arranged alphabetically by the state with which they were associated at the time they entered Confederate military service. Their grades and their antebellum military experience are indicated by the following symbols:

General Officer Grades		Known Antebellum Military Experience
G	full general	1 military education
LG	lieutenant general	2 professional military service (excluding men in groups 1 and 3)
MG	major general	
BG	brigadier general	3 Mexican War service (excluding men in groups 1 and 2)
		4 Indian wars/Texas war for independence (excluding men in groups 1 and 2)
		5 state militia service
		6 other

It is probable that more thorough knowledge about some of the more obscure generals would lead to an increase in the number of men with pre–Civil War military experience—especially for men with militia service. Such a change, however, probably would not necessitate major changes in the numbers reflecting the differences between the two great Rebel armies.

Appendix

ALABAMA

No full generals; one lieutenant general; six major generals; twenty-seven brigadier generals.

Allen, William M. (MG)

Baker, Alpheus (BG)

Battle, Cullen A. (BG)

Cantey, James (BG) 3

Clanton, James H. (BG) 3

Clayton, Henry D. (MG)

Deas, Zachariah C. (BG) 3

Deshler, James (BG) 1

Forney, John H. (MG) 3

Forney, William H. (BG) 3

Fry, Birkett D. (BG) 1

Garrott, Isham W. (BG)

Gorgas, Josiah (BG) 1

Gracie, Archibald J. (BG) 1, 5

Holtzclaw, James T. (BG)

Johnston, George D. (BG)

Kelly, John H. (BG) 1

Law, Evander M. (BG) 1

Leadbetter, Danville (BG) 1, 5

Longstreet, James (LG) 1

Moody, Young M. (BG)

Morgan, John T. (BG)

O'Neal, Edward A. (BG)

Perry, William F. (BG)

Pettus, Edmund W. (BG)

Roddey, Philip D. (BG)

Rodes, Robert E. (MG) 1

Sanders, John C. C. (BG)

Shelly, Charles M. (BG)

Tracy, Edward D. (BG)

Walker, Leroy P. (BG) 5

Wheeler, Joseph (MG) 1

Withers, Jones M. (MG) 1, 5

Wood, Sterling A. M. (BG)

ARKANSAS

No full generals; no lieutenant generals; four major generals; fifteen brigadier generals.

Armstrong, Frank C. (BG) 2

Barton, Seth M. (BG) 1

Beale, William N. R. (BG) 1

Churchill, Thomas J. (MG) 3

Cleburne, Patrick R. (MG) 2

Dockery, Thomas P. (BG)

Fagan, James F. (MG) 3

Govan, Daniel C. (BG)

Hawthorn, Alexander T. (BG)

Hindman, Thomas C. (MG) 3

McIntosh, James M. (BG) 1

McNair, Evander (BG) 3

McRae, Dandridge (BG)

Pike, Albert (BG) 3

Polk, Lucius E. (BG)

Reynolds, Daniel H. (BG)

Roane, John S. (BG) 3

Rust, Albert (BG)

Tappan, James C. (BG)

Appendix

FLORIDA

One full general; no lieutenant generals; three major generals; nine brigadier generals.

Anderson, James Patton (MG) 3, 5
Brevard, Theodore W. (BG)
Bullock, Robert (BG) 4
Davis, William G. M. (BG)
Finegan, Joseph (BG)
Finley, Jesse J. (BG) 4
Loring, William W. (MG) 2

Miller, William (BG) 3
Perry, Edward A. (BG)
Shoup, Francis A. (BG) 1
Smith, Edmund K. (G) 1
Smith, Martin L. (MG) 1
Walker, William S. (BG) 2

GEORGIA

No full generals; one lieutenant general; seven major generals; thirty-four brigadier generals.

Alexander, E. Porter (BG) 1
Anderson, George T. (BG) 2
Anderson, Robert H. (BG) 1
Benning, Henry L. (BG)
Boggs, William R. (BG) 1
Browne, William M. (BG) 2
Bryan, Goode (BG) 1
Cobb, Howell (MG)
Cobb, Thomas R. R. (BG)
Colquitt, Alfred H. (BG) 3
Cook, Philip (BG) 4
Cumming, Alfred (BG) 1
Doles, George P. (BG) 5
DuBose, Dudley M. (BG)
Evans, Clement A. (BG)
Gardner, William M. (BG) 1
Gartrell, Lucius J. (BG)
Girardey, Victor J. B. (BG)
Gordon, John B. (MG)
Hardee, William J. (LG) 1
Iverson, Alfred (BG) 2

Jackson, Henry R. (BG) 3
Jackson, John K. (BG) 5
Lawton, Alexander R. (BG) 1
McLaws, Lafayette (MG) 1
Mercer, Hugh W. (BG) 1
St. John, Isaac M. (BG)
Semmes, John P. (BG) 5
Simms, James P. (BG)
Smith, William D. (BG) 1
Sorrell, Gilbert M. (BG) 5
Stovall, Marcellus A. (BG) 1
Thomas, Bryan M. (BG) 1
Thomas, Edward L. (BG) 3
Toombs, Robert A. (BG)
Twiggs, David E. (MG) 2
Walker, William H. T. (MG) 1
Wayne, Henry C. (BG) 1
Wilson, Claudius C. (BG)
Wofford, William T. (BG) 3
Wright, Ambrose R. (MG)
Young, Pierce M. B. (MG) 1

INDIAN TERRITORY

One brigadier general.
Watie, Stand (BG)

KENTUCKY

One full general; one lieutenant general; three major generals; seventeen brigadier generals.

Breckinridge, John C. (MG) 3
Buckner, Simon B. (LG) 1, 5
Buford, Abraham (BG) 1
Cosby, George B. (BG) 1
Crittenden, George B. (MG) 1
Duke, Basil W. (BG)
Grayson, John B. (BG) 1
Hanson, Roger W. (BG) 3
Hawes, James M. (BG) 1
Helm, Benjamin H. (BG) 1
Hodge, George B. (BG) 1

Hood, John Bell (G) 1
Johnson, Adam R. (BG) 4
Lewis, Joseph H. (BG)
Lyon, Hylan B. (BG) 1
Marshall, Humphrey (BG) 1
Morgan, John H. (BG) 3
Preston, William (BG) 3
Smith, Gustavus W. (MG) 1
Taylor, Thomas H. (BG) 3
Tilghman, Lloyd (BG) 1
Williams, John S. (BG) 3

LOUISIANA

Two full generals; two lieutenant generals; two major generals; twenty-one brigadier generals.

Adams, Daniel W. (BG)
Allen, Henry W. (BG) 4
Beauregard, P. G. T. (G) 1
Blanchard, Albert G. (BG) 1
Bragg, Braxton (G) 1
Duncan, Johnson K. (BG) 1
Gardner, Franklin (MG) 1
Gibson, Randall L. (BG)
Gladden, Adley H. (BG) 3, 4
Gray, Henry (BG)
Hays, Harry T. (BG) 3
Hebert, Louis (BG) 1
Hebert, Paul O. (BG) 1
Higgins, Edward (BG) 2

Liddell, St. John R. (BG) 1
Mouton, Jean J. A. (BG) 1, 5
Nicholls, Francis R. T. (BG) 1
Peck, William R. (BG)
Polignac, Camille Armand (MG) 2
Polk, Leonidas (LG) 1
Scott, Thomas M. (BG)
Sibley, Henry H. (BG) 1
Stafford, Leroy H. (BG) 3
Starke, William E. (BG)
Taylor, Richard (LG) 6
Thomas, Allen (BG)
York, Zebulon (BG)

Appendix

MARYLAND

No full generals; no lieutenant generals; three major generals; six brigadier generals.

Archer, James J. (BG) 2
Elzy, Arnold (MG) 1
Johnson, Bradley T. (BG)
Lovell, Mansfield (MG) 1
Mackall, William W. (BG) 1

Steuart, George H. (BG) 1
Trimble, Isaac (MG) 1
Winder, Charles S. (BG) 1
Winder, John H. (BG) 1

MISSISSIPPI

No full generals; no lieutenant generals; five major generals; twenty-four brigadier generals.

Adams, William W. (BG) 2
Baldwin, William E. (BG) 5
Barksdale, William (BG) 3
Benton, Samuel (BG)
Brandon, William L. (BG) 5
Brantley, William F. (BG)
Chalmers, James R. (BG)
Clark, Charles (BG) 3
Cooper, Douglas H. (BG) 3
Davis, Joseph R. (BG)
Featherston, Winfield S. (BG) 4
Ferguson, Samuel W. (BG) 1
Frazer, John W. (BG) 1
French, Samuel G. (MG) 1
Gholson, Samuel J. (BG)

Griffith, Richard (BG) 3
Harris, Nathaniel H. (BG)
Humphreys, Benjamin G. (BG) 1
Lowrey, Mark P. (BG) 3
Lowry, Robert (BG)
Martin, William T. (MG)
Posey, Carnot (BG) 3
Sears, Claudius W. (BG) 1
Sharp, Jacob H. (BG)
Starke, Peter B. (BG)
Tucker, William F. (BG)
Van Dorn, Earl (MG) 1
Walthall, Edward C. (MG)
Whiting, William H. C. (MG) 1

MISSOURI

No full generals; no lieutenant generals; four major generals; eight brigadier generals.

Bowen, John S. (MG) 1
Clark, John B., Jr. (BG)
Cockrell, Francis M. (BG)
Frost, Daniel M. (BG) 1, 5
Green, Martin E. (BG)
Little, Henry L. (BG) 2

Marmaduke, John S. (MG) 1
Parsons, Mosby M. (BG) 3
Price, Sterling (MG) 3
Shelby, Joseph O. (BG)
Slack, William Y. (BG) 3
Walker, John (MG) 2

Appendix

NORTH CAROLINA

No full generals; two lieutenant generals; five major generals; twenty-six brigadier generals.

Anderson, George B. (BG) 1
Baker, Laurence S. (BG) 1
Barringer, Rufus (BG)
Barry, John Decatur (BG)
Branch, Lawrence O'B. (BG)
Clingman, Thomas L. (BG)
Cooke, John R. (BG) 2
Cox, William R. (BG) 5
Daniel, Junius (BG) 1
Gatlin, Richard C. (BG) 1
Gilmer, Jeremy F. (MG) 1
Godwin, Archibald C. (BG)
Gordon, James B. (BG)
Grimes, Bryan (MG)
Hill, Daniel H. (LG) 1
Hoke, Robert F. (MG) 1
Holmes, Theophilus H. (LG) 1

Johnston, Robert D. (BG) 5
Kirkland, William W. (BG) 1
Lane, James H. (BG) 2
Leventhrope, Collett (BG) 2
Lewis, William G. (BG) 5
MacRae, William (BG)
Martin, James G. (BG) 1
Pender, William D. (MG) 1
Rains, Gabriel J. (BG) 1
Ramseur, Stephen D. (MG) 1
Ransom, Matt W. (BG)
Ransom, Robert, Jr. (BG) 1
Roberts, William P. (BG)
Scales, Alfred M. (BG)
Toon, Thomas F. (BG)
Vance, Robert B. (BG)

SOUTH CAROLINA

No full generals; three lieutenant generals; four major generals; twenty-eight brigadier generals.

Anderson, Richard H. (LG) 1
Bee, Barnard E. (BG) 1
Bonham, Milledge L. (BG) 3, 4
Bratton, John (BG)
Butler, Matthew C. (MG)
Capers, Ellison (BG) 1
Chesnut, James (BG)
Conner, James (BG) 5
Drayton, Thomas F. (BG) 1
Dunovant, John (BG) 2
Elliott, Stephen (BG) 5
Evans, Nathan G. (BG) 1
Gary, Martin W. (BG)
Gist, States R. (BG) 5
Gregg, Maxcy (BG) 3

Hagood, Johnson (BG) 1, 5
Hampton, Wade (LG)
Huger, Benjamin (MG) 1
Jenkins, Micah (BG) 1
Jones, David R. (MG) 1
Kennedy, John G. (BG)
Kershaw, Joseph B. (MG) 3
Lee, Stephen D. (LG) 1
Logan, Thomas M. (BG)
McGowan, Samuel (BG) 3, 5
Manigault, Arthur M. (BG) 3, 5
Northrop, Lucius B. (BG) 1
Perrin, Abner M. (BG)
Pettigrew, James J. (BG) 5
Preston, John S. (BG)

Ripley, Roswell S. (BG) 1
Stevens, Clement H. (BG)
Trapier, James H. (BG) 1, 5

Villepigue, John B. (BG) 1
Wallace, William H. (BG)

TENNESSEE

No full generals; two lieutenant generals; eight major generals; thirty brigadier generals.

Adams, John (BG) 1
Anderson, Samuel R. (BG) 3
Bate, William B. (MG) 3
Bell, Tyree H. (BG)
Brown, John C. (MG)
Campbell, Alexander W. (BG)
Carroll, William H. (BG) 5
Carter, John C. (BG)
Cheatham, Benjamin F. (MG) 3, 5
Davidson, Henry B. (BG) 1
Dibrell, George G. (BG)
Donelson, Daniel S. (MG) 1, 5
Forrest, Nathan B. (LG)
Gordon, George W. (BG)
Hatton, Robert H. (BG)
Hill, Benjamin J. (BG)
Humes, W. Y. C. (MG) 1
Jackson, Alfred E. (BG)
Jackson, William H. (BG) 1
Johnson, Bushrod R. (MG) 1, 5

McComb, William (BG)
McCown, John P. (MG) 1
Maney, George E. (BG) 3
Palmer, Joseph B. (BG)
Pillow, Gideon J. (BG) 3
Quarles, William A. (BG)
Rains, James E. (BG)
Richardson, Robert V. (BG)
Smith, James A. (BG) 1
Smith, Preston (BG)
Smith, Thomas B. (BG) 1
Stewart, Alexander P. (LG) 1
Strahl, Otho F. (BG)
Tyler, Robert C. (BG)
Vaughan, Alfred J., Jr. (BG) 1
Vaughn, John C. (BG) 3
Walker, Lucius M. (BG) 1
Wilcox, Cadmus M. (MG) 1
Wright, Marcus J. (BG) 5
Zollicoffer, Felix (BG) 4

TEXAS

One full general; no lieutenant generals; one major general; twenty-seven brigadier generals.

Bee, Hamilton P. (BG) 3, 5
Ector, Matthew D. (BG)
Gano, Richard M. (BG) 4
Granbury, Hiram B. (BG)
Green, Thomas (BG) 3, 4
Greer, Elkanah (BG) 3
Gregg, John (BG)

Hardeman, William P. (BG) 3, 4
Harrison, James E. (BG)
Hogg, Joseph L. (BG) 3, 5
Johnston, Albert S. (G) 1
Lane, Walter P. (BG) 3, 4
McCulloch, Ben (BG) 3, 4
McCulloch, Henry E. (BG) 3

Major, James P. (BG) 1

Maxey, Samuel B. (BG) 1

Moore, John C. (BG)

Nelson, Allison (BG) 3, 4

Robertson, Felix H. (BG) 1

Robertson, Jerome B. (BG) 4

Ross, Lawrence S. (BG) 4

Scurry, William R. (BG) 3

Steele, William (BG) 1

Waterhouse, Richard (BG) 3

Waul, Thomas N. (BG)

Wharton, John A. (MG)

Whitfield, John W. (BG) 3

Wigfall, Louis T. (BG) 5

Young, William H. (BG)

VIRGINIA

Three full generals; five lieutenant generals; seventeen major generals; fifty-four brigadier generals.

Anderson, Joseph R. (BG) 1

Armistead, Lewis A. (BG) 1

Ashby, Turner (BG)

Beale, Richard L. T. (BG)

Cabell, William L. (BG) 1

Chambliss, John R. (BG) 1, 5

Chilton, Robert H. (BG) 1

Cocke, Philip St. G. (BG) 1

Colston, Raleigh E. (BG) 1

Cooper, Samuel (G) 1

Corse, Montgomery D. (BG) 3, 5

Dearing, James (BG) 1

de Lagnel, Julius A. (BG) 2

Early, Jubal A. (LG) 1

Echols, John (BG) 1

Ewell, Richard S. (LG) 1

Field, Charles W. (MG) 1

Floyd, John B. (BG)

Garland, Samuel (BG) 1, 5

Garnett, Richard B. (BG) 1

Garnett, Robert S. (BG) 1

Goggin, James M. (BG) 1

Heth, Henry (MG) 1

Hill, Ambrose P. (LG) 1

Hunton, Eppa (BG) 5

Imboden, John D. (BG)

Jackson, Thomas J. (LG) 1

Jackson, William L. (BG)

Jenkins, Albert G. (BG)

Johnson, Edward (MG) 1

Johnston, Joseph E. (G) 1

Jones, John M. (BG) 1

Jones, John R. (BG) 1, 5

Jones, Samuel (MG) 1

Jones, William E. (BG) 1

Jordan, Thomas (BG) 1

Kemper, James L. (MG) 3

Lee, Edwin G. (BG)

Lee, Fitzhugh (MG) 1

Lee, George W. C. (MG) 1

Lee, Robert E. (G) 1

Lee, William H. F. (MG) 2

Lilley, Robert D. (BG)

Lomax, Lunsford L. (MG) 1

Long, Armistead L. (BG) 1

McCausland, John (BG) 1

Magruder, John B. (MG) 1

Mahone, William (MG) 1

Maury, Dabney H. (MG) 1

Moore, Patrick T. (BG) 5

Page, Richard L. (BG) 2

Paxton, Elisha F. (BG)

Payne, William H. F. (BG) 1

Pegram, John (BG) 1

Pemberton, John C. (LG) 1

Pendleton, William N. (BG) 1

Pickett, George E. (MG) 1
Pryor, Roger A. (BG)
Randolph, George W. (BG) 2, 5
Reynolds, Alexander W. (BG) 1
Robertson, Beverly H. (BG) 1
Rosser, Thomas L. (MG) 1
Ruggles, Daniel (BG) 1
Slaughter, James E. (BG) 1
Smith, William (MG)
Stevens, Walter H. (BG) 1
Stevenson, Carter L. (MG) 1
Stuart, James E. B. (MG) 1

Taliaferro, William B. (BG) 3, 5
Terrill, James B. (BG) 5
Terry, William (BG) 5
Terry, William R. (BG) 1
Walker, Harry H. (BG) 1
Walker, James A. (BG) 1
Walker, Reuben L. (BG) 1
Weisiger, David A. (BG) 3, 5
Wharton, Gabriel C. (BG) 1
Wickham, Williams C. (BG) 5
Wise, Henry A. (BG)

Notes

This book was planned and written to appeal to the general reader as well as to the historian. Accordingly, the scholarly apparatus is presented as simply as possible. To keep the text uncluttered, the sources for quotations and other factual information are summarized in notes following sections of the book to which they pertain.

CHAPTER ONE

1. Most of the Confederate armies are conveniently listed in Boatner, *Civil War Dictionary*, p. 26. The Army of New River and the Army of East Florida were so minuscule that they escaped even Boatner's eagle eye. For record of their existence see United States War Department, *War of the Rebellion*, ser. I, vol. 12, p. 491 (hereafter cited as *OR*, with all references to volumes in series I); and the February and March 1864 documents in the compiled service record of Colonel Charles Colcock Jones, Jr., in the Compiled Service Records of Confederate Staff Officers and Non-Regimental Enlisted Men, National Archives. Harwell and Racine, eds., *Fiery Trail*, p. 187.

2. *OR*, vol. 20, pt. 2, p. 411; Freeman, *Lee's Lieutenants*, 1:49n.

3. Swinton, *Campaigns*, pp. 1, 3, 11, 14, 16. For a rare early exception to the overemphasis on operations in the Virginia theater see Fiske, *Mississippi Valley in the Civil War*. Even Fiske, however, was at least partially seduced by the charms of Virginia. In addition to his obeisance to Lee that was described in the Preface, he wrote that "in Virginia Lee's power of resistance seemed interminable" and of the "spell" the Old Dominion "cast upon the imagination of European statesmen" and that in 1865 Virginia fell "vanquished but not humiliated" after the Yankees had cut away the rest of the Confederacy (ibid., pp. ix, 3–4, 317, 320–23, 331).

4. Horn, *Army of Tennessee*, p. xi.

5. Only Longstreet's role at Gettysburg was discussed in the textbooks. His doings at Chickamauga and Knoxville were not mentioned.

6. Tindall, *America*, pp. 627–40, 653–65; Sellers et al., *Synopsis of American History*, pp. 195–96, 200–201; Norton et al., *A People and a Nation*, brief ed., pp. 211–13, 221–24; and ibid., 2d ed., 1:383–87, 404–5, 410–13;

O'Connor, *Disunited States*, chaps. 10–12. The percentages were determined by measuring the inches of column text devoted to each theater.

7. U.S. Civil War Centennial Commission, *Civil War*, p. 27; Stein, ed., *Random House Dictionary*, pp. 41, 192, 231, 380, 513.

8. Freeman, *Lee's Lieutenants*, 1:701–25. I am indebted to Grady McWhiney for the observation about historians reading the history of the entire South as that of Virginia writ large. McWhiney drew the analogy from a historian who observed that the history of Great Britain was the history of England imposed upon the non-English peoples of the British Isles (McWhiney, conversations with author, Murfreesboro, Tennessee, 5–7 May 1983).

9. Henderson, *Stonewall Jackson*, p. 605.

10. It would be pointless to cite here all of the biographies that have been written about the generals. Relevant books will be cited later at more appropriate points. For a listing of many of these biographies see McPherson, *Ordeal by Fire*, p. 677. More recent works are listed in *Civil War Book Exchange & Collectors Newspaper*, the book review sections of the professional historical journals, and the advertisements and reviews in *Civil War Times Illustrated, Blue & Gray*, and *Virginia Country's Civil War Quarterly*.

11. Siepel, *Rebel*; Jones, *Ranger Mosby*; Bean, *Stonewall's Man*; Davis, *Boy Colonel of the Confederacy*; Hassler, *Colonel John Pelham*; Milham, *Gallant Pelham*; Krick, *Lee's Colonels*. In this edition of his biographical register Krick has added a list of field grade officers who served with Confederate commands outside the Army of Northern Virginia. For an example of the Howard books see Frye, *2d Virginia Infantry*.

Some other Southern states have published rosters of their Confederate troops. See, for example, Booth, comp., *Records of Louisiana Confederate Soldiers*; [Tennessee] Civil War Centennial Commission, *Tennesseans in the Civil War*; and Henderson, comp., *Rosters of Confederate Soldiers of Georgia*.

North Carolina's published records come closest to matching those available on Virginia troops, but the Tarheel efforts are not complete histories with maps and photographs. Because almost all of North Carolina's Rebel troops served in Virginia, publication of that state's records simply increases the already wide gulf between the information about the eastern and western armies. See Clark, ed., *Histories of the Several Regiments and Battalions from North Carolina*; and Manarin and Jordan, eds., *North Carolina Troops*.

12. McWhiney, *Braxton Bragg and Confederate Defeat*.

13. Alexander, *Military Memoirs*; Sorrel, *Recollections*; Douglas, *I Rode With Stonewall*; Cooke, *Wearing of the Gray*; Eggleston, *Rebel's Recollections*. Cooke also wrote biographies of Robert E. Lee and Stonewall Jackson, along with several novels romanticizing the Army of Northern Virginia, including *Surry of Eagle's Nest* and *Mohun*.

14. See, for example, Norton, *Attack and Defense of Little Round Top*; Stewart, *Pickett's Charge*; Davis, *Battle of New Market*; Jones, *Eight Hours before Richmond*; and Pfanz, *Gettysburg*. Sommers, *Richmond Redeemed*, is the best battle study in American historiography; it ranks with the best books on any facet of American history.

For recent good works on some of the western battles see Hewitt, *Port Hudson* and Cooling, *Forts Henry and Donelson*. See also the books by McDonough, *Shiloh*; *Stones River*, *Chattanooga*; with Connelly, *Five Tragic Hours*; and with Jones, *War So Terrible*.

15. Connelly's catalog is in *Army of the Heartland*, pp. viii–ix. See also Connelly, "The Image and the General"; and Connelly and Bellows, *God and General Longstreet*, chaps. 2 and 3. The Arkansan's comments are in Civil War Round Table Associates *Digest*, p. 2.

CHAPTER TWO

1. On Maryland's role during the war see Manakee, *Maryland in the Civil War*; Baker, *Politics of Continuity*; Wright, *Secession Movement in the Middle Atlantic States*, pp. 21–73; and Clark, "Suppression and Control of Maryland," pp. 241–71.

2. On Kentucky see Coulter, *Civil War and Readjustment in Kentucky*; Townsend, *Lincoln and the Bluegrass*; Harrison, *Civil War in Kentucky*; and *OR*, 4:175–81. Connelly and Jones discuss the "Kentucky bloc" in *Politics of Command*, pp. 72–82. The *Richmond Whig*, 11 Sept. 1861, published several glowing accounts of pro-Confederate sentiment in Kentucky. For a late, equally glowing, assessment of Rebel prospects in the Bluegrass see the *Mobile Advertiser*, n.d., quoted in the *Columbus* (Ga.) *Daily Enquirer*, 17 Dec. 1864. Cameron's statements are discussed in the *Richmond Daily Dispatch*, 23 Dec. 1861; Coulter, *Civil War and Readjustment in Kentucky*, p. 156; and Cornish, *Sable Arm*, pp. 21–24. The Rebel Bluegrass government is covered in Lowell Harrison's chapter "Kentucky," in Yearns, ed., *Confederate Governors*, pp. 83–90.

The situation in Kentucky was considerably more complex than the summary I have provided indicates. Most Unionists were willing to cooperate with those who honestly favored neutrality because by so doing they kept the state out of the Confederacy. The North, too, established enlistment stations for Kentuckians and sent surreptitious help to its friends in the state. President Abraham Lincoln was wise enough to realize that a "neutral" Kentucky in the Union was a great asset to the Northern cause, and he was careful not to do anything that might push the state into the Confederacy even as he worked successfully to hold it for the Federal government.

3. On Missouri see McElroy, *Struggle for Missouri*; Anderson, *Rebellion in Missouri*; Parrish, *History of Missouri*; Parrish, "Missouri," in Yearns, ed., *Confederate Governors*, pp. 130–39; and Parrish, *Turbulent Partnership*.

4. Many authors have commented on the differences between the eastern and western rivers. See, for example, Milligan, *Gunboats down the Mississippi*, pp. xxii–xxiii; Walker, "Building a Tennessee Army"; and McPherson, *Ordeal by Fire*, pp. 185–86. The comment from the *Savannah Republican* is quoted in the *Atlanta Southern Confederacy*, 20 Mar. 1862. Reed, *Combined Operations*, p. xvi, discusses the value of rivers as safe, secure lines of supply. I am indebted to Michael Hughes, of Ada, Oklahoma, for his comments about the relatively greater crookedness of the Georgia rivers and their numerous fords. Hughes made these remarks at a panel discussion on the Atlanta Campaign at the Congress of Civil War Round Tables held at Marietta, Georgia, on 2 October 1986.

5. On the war in the mountains see Temple, *East Tennessee and the Civil War*; Ambler, *History of West Virginia*; Curry, *House Divided*; and Reed, *Combined Operations*, p. 38.

6. These data and those given later in the text are from the 1860 census or from the sources listed in this note. For some examples of writings emphasizing Northern economic superiority see Randall, *Civil War and Reconstruction*, p. 83; Randall and Donald, *Civil War and Reconstruction*, pp. 1–13; McPherson, *Ordeal by Fire*, pp. 5–35; O'Connor, *Disunited States*, pp. 158–60; and Robert H. Jones, *Disrupted Decades*, pp. 10, 48. The theme of Northern economic strength permeates Davis, *Imperiled Union*. For a textbook example see Gruver, *American History*, 1:499–500. On the railroads see Black, *Railroads of the Confederacy*. Cappon, "Trend of the Southern Iron Industry," contains interesting material on antebellum economic development. An excellent overall summary with many relevant statistics, although not per se a comparison of North and South, is in North, *Economic Growth of the United States*, esp. pp. 122–76.

7. This classification of states is arbitrary, but the same divisions will be used in Chapter 6 to compare troops and military units that served in the Army of Tennessee with those that served in the Army of Northern Virginia. This classification of states grew from a study of the makeup of the two armies. It was applied later to the economic data.

8. On the Virginia railroads see Johnston, *Virginia Railroads*. For the connecting track through Richmond see ibid., p. 56, and *Richmond Daily Dispatch*, 9 Dec. 1861. Black's *Railroads of the Confederacy* has a map showing all of the Rebels' rail lines.

9. It might be argued that the figures used in the text are misleading and that none of the Trans-Mississippi states should be included in the "West." It should be remembered, however, that the Army of Tennessee was origi-

nally the Army of *the* (my emphasis) Mississippi; that the Southerners' original defense scheme in the West was built around Department Number 2, which included part of Louisiana, western Mississippi, West Tennessee, and eastern Arkansas; and that the command in the West was soon afterward extended to embrace the entire area between the Appalachians and the Ozarks except for the Gulf Coast. For these reasons it seemed better, at least when discussing the early years of the war, to define the West as I have done and, perhaps, to omit Texas.

One could argue that after the spring of 1862 the Army of Tennessee had no meaningful contact with the Trans-Mississippi and that, therefore, only the states where it campaigned should be considered. This assumption would reduce the West to Tennessee, Mississippi, Alabama, and, perhaps, Georgia. Here again, several things should be kept in mind. First, for much of the time after the spring of 1862 there were two large Confederate forces in the West—the Army of Tennessee and the army that defended Vicksburg—and the region's economic resources had to be divided between them. Second, after the early months of 1862 the Army of Tennessee had no real connection with large chunks of the Volunteer State that were under permanent Federal occupation. Third, the industrial production of Virginia alone in 1860 exceeded the combined total for Alabama, Mississippi, and Tennessee by 44 percent. If Georgia is considered a western state, the western total exceeds Virginia's by only $1,439,923. Even counting Georgia with the West, the East as a whole still outproduced the West by almost $24 million (45.8 percent).

Of course, West Virginia presents problems in calculating the Old Dominion's economic and population resources. Not the least of these problems is the question of what counties should be counted as West Virginia. Should the area include all fifty counties that were eventually taken from Virginia to form the new state? Should it be limited to the thirty-two counties that were represented at the June–August 1861 Wheeling Convention? Should the West Virginia data include Jefferson and Berkeley counties—area that was not in the original plan for the new state? When did each of the Mountain State's counties pass from Confederate control?

The fifty counties that wound up in West Virginia had a white population in 1860 of 355,587; 21,088 slaves; and 1,095 manufacturing establishments with an annual production valued at $9,009,125. (There were eleven Virginia counties—three in the eastern part of the state and eight in the western—for which no reports on manufacturing were received by the Census Office.) Even without counting any of the West Virginia area, Virginia's 1860 industrial production exceeded that of second-place Tennessee by $23,655,774 (131.5 percent).

The Confederate supply system, of course, was more complex than merely having the East supply one army and the West another. See Goff, *Confederate Supply*, and Chapter 4 of this book.

Some of the sources cited in note 6 use slightly different figures for some of the examples. One could poke around in the census data, local and state histories, newspapers, and other records and come up with still other numbers. One could also try to arrive at production figures for 1863 and 1864, by which time the Rebels had created large munitions facilities at various points in both the eastern and western Confederacy but had also lost large areas of the territory they held in 1861, especially in the West. One could even put fresh batteries into one's calculator. None of these acts, however, would alter the fundamental fact that, throughout the war, the eastern states of the Confederacy were far better prepared to provide economic support for an army than were those in the West—no matter how that region is defined. In modern terms, the North was a superpower, the eastern Confederacy a third-rate power, and the Confederate West belonged in the fourth world.

For all these reasons it seemed better simply to use some of the data to illustrate the point and not to wander off into the labyrinthine morass of arguing over individual numbers.

CHAPTER THREE

1. For discussions of the battle and the reasons for its outcome see Coddington, *Gettysburg Campaign*; Freeman, *Lee's Lieutenants*, 3:1–205; Hassler, *A. P. Hill*, pp. 236–38; Vandiver, *Their Tattered Flags*, pp. 223–24; Robertson, *A. P. Hill*; Connelly and Bellows, *God and General Longstreet*, pp. 30–38; Aliyetti, "From Brandy Station to Gettysburg"; and Green, "A. P. Hill's Manic Depression." A convenient collection of writings on the controversy is to be found in Brown, "Lee at Gettysburg"; Krick, " 'I Consider Him a Humbug' "; Krolick, "Lee and Longstreet at Gettysburg"; Hassler, "A. P. Hill at Gettysburg"; Gallagher, "In the Shadow of Stonewall Jackson"; and Georg, "Where Was Pickett?"

2. Fiske, *Mississippi Valley in the Civil War*, pp. 315–16.

3. Hassler, *Commanders of the Army of the Potomac*, pp. 3, 5, 6, 21, 246; Williams, *Lincoln Finds a General*, 1:67, 91, 94; Davis, *Battle at Bull Run*, pp. 10, 35–36; T. Harry Williams, *Lincoln and His Generals*, p. 19.

4. Hassler, *Commanders of the Army of the Potomac*, pp. 28–31, 247–49, 262; Williams, *Lincoln Finds a General*, 1:127, 148, 155, 249; 2:307, 479; Catton, *This Hallowed Ground*, p. 87; McPherson, *Ordeal by Fire*, pp. 243, 255n; Davis, *Deep Waters of the Proud*, p. 157.

5. Hassler, *Commanders of the Army of the Potomac*, pp. 59–62, 67–68, 72, 249–50.

6. Ibid., pp. 99–101, 107, 122, 252; Williams, *Lincoln and His Generals*, pp. 180, 201–2; Thomas, *American War and Peace*, p. 104; Fair, *From the Jaws of Victory*, pp. 5, 254–55.

7. Hassler, *Commanders of the Army of the Potomac*, pp. 126, 128–33, 255–56, 262; Williams, *Lincoln Finds a General*, 2:604; Fair, *From the Jaws of Victory*, pp. 5, 254–55; Robert Krick to author, 10 June 1987.

8. Hassler, *Commanders of the Army of the Potomac*, pp. 161–64, 257–58; Williams, *Lincoln Finds a General*, 2:677–80; and Krolick, "George Gordon Meade."

9. Adams, *Our Masters the Rebels*; Watson, *Cavalier*. For other general accounts of the myth see Taylor, *Cavalier and Yankee*; Floan, *The South in Northern Eyes*; Fishwick, *Virginia*. For information on the agrarian myth and its military implications see Ward, *Andrew Jackson*. "SOUTHWESTERN" letter is in the *Charleston Mercury*, 6 Nov. 1861. For an example of Confederate respect for the fighting qualities of the western Yankees see the *Little Rock Democrat*, 13 Mar. 1862, quoted in the *Savannah Daily Republican*, 24 Mar. 1862. For an excellent description of some of the western Federals see Glatthaar, *March to the Sea*. McDowell is quoted in Davis, *Deep Waters of the Proud*, p. 68.

10. Ambrose, *Halleck*. See also Williams, *Lincoln and His Generals*, pp. 136–38. Halleck's role and the strategy he successfully advocated are well described in Hattaway and Jones, *How the North Won*, esp. pp. 286, 292–93, 333–34, 348, 350, 371–72, 385, 426, 516–18, 528, 569–70, 593–94, 657, 663, 669, 685, 687, 689–91, 695. Scott described the "Anaconda plan" in a letter to McClellan in *OR*, vol. 51, pt. 1, pp. 369–70. See also ibid., pp. 386–87. Williams, *Lincoln Finds a General*, 2:17–18; Catton, *This Hallowed Ground*, pp. 86–88; Connelly and Jones, *Politics of Command*, p. 21; McFeely, *Grant*, p. 175. Basic biographical information on Halleck, as well as all the other Federal generals, is in Warner, *Generals in Blue*.

CHAPTER FOUR

1. For some typical comments on the removal of the capital see Coulter, *Confederate States of America*, pp. 98–102; Nevins, *Improvised War*, pp. 101–2; Davis, *Deep Waters of the Proud*, pp. 67, 90–92; Yearns, *Confederate Congress*, pp. 12–13; Wert, "Confederate Strategy," p. 44; and Vandiver, *Their Tattered Flags*, pp. 56–57.

2. For comments on the problems arising from the departmental system

see Wert, "Confederate Strategy"; Connelly, _Army of the Heartland_, pp. 11–12; Connelly, _Autumn of Glory_, pp. 6–7, 157–58, 377–81, 434; Connelly and Jones, _Politics of Command_, pp. 87–136 and passim; Vandiver, _Rebel Brass_, pp. 29–37; McMurry, " 'The _Enemy_ at Richmond' "; and McMurry, "The Opening Phase of the 1864 Campaign in the West." Nevins's comment on interior lines is in _Improvised War_, p. 96. See also Roland, "Generalship of Robert E. Lee," pp. 32–33.

3. On Confederate supply matters in general see Goff, _Confederate Supply_; pp. 4, 56, 58–59, 78–83, 185, and 188 contain specific comments on the Army of Tennessee and its logistical difficulties. See also Connelly, _Army of the Heartland_, pp. 11–12, and _Autumn of Glory_, pp. 7, 17–18, 113–15, 157; Walker, "Building a Tennessee Army," pp. 110–11; Johnston, _Narrative of Military Operations_, pp. 374–76; McDonough, "Cold Days in Hell."

4. Meade is quoted in Hassler, _Commanders of the Army of the Potomac_, p. 219.

CHAPTER FIVE

1. For a history of one such volunteer unit see Smith, _Chatham Artillery_, and Jones, _Historical Sketch of the Chatham Artillery_. Myers, ed., _Children of Pride_, contains many letters from C. C. Jones, Jr., written between 1856 and 1862, when he was a member of the Chatham Artillery. These documents give an excellent picture of many of the unit's activities. Other accounts of late antebellum volunteer military units are to be found in Wallace, _1st Virginia Infantry_, pp. 1–9 and 11, and in many issues of the _Savannah Daily Morning News_ of the late 1850s. For comments on prewar artillery units in the East and their nearly total absence from the western states of the Confederacy, see Daniel, _Cannoneers in Gray_, pp. 7–8.

2. Boney, _John Letcher of Virginia_, pp. 105–17, 120–25; Shanks, _Secession Movement in Virginia_, pp. 96, 147–48, 254; Couper, _One Hundred Years at V.M.I._, 1:310, 345, 2:41–42; Freeman, _R. E. Lee_, 1:463, 472–526; Dowdey, _Lee_, pp. 142–50; Nevins, _Improvised War_, p. 116.

3. The best general treatment of the Tennessee state army is in Connelly, _Army of the Heartland_, pp. 25–45. On Pillow see ibid., pp. 47–48; McDonough, "Cold Days in Hell," p. 51; Grant, _Personal Memoirs_, 1:172–73, 309; Russell, _Diary_, p. 162; Davis, _Deep Waters of the Proud_, p. 116; Robertson, _A. P. Hill_, p. 18.

4. The best accounts of Lee's work in preparing the Virginia state forces are in Freeman, _Lee_, 1:491–526, and Dowdey, _Lee_, pp. 145–55.

5. Connelly, _Army of the Heartland_, pp. 25–45; Russell, _Diary_, pp. 161–

62; Connelly, *Civil War Tennessee*, pp. 3–4, 18; Horn, ed. and comp., *Tennessee's War*, pp. 17–18.

6. Boney, *John Letcher of Virginia*, pp. 123–24; Freeman, *Lee*, 1:493.

7. Connelly, *Army of the Heartland*, pp. 30–31; Daniel, *Cannoneers in Gray*, p. 6.

8. Connelly, *Army of the Heartland*, p. 43.

9. Connelly, *Army of the Heartland*, pp. 32, 47–49; Freeman, *Lee* 1:469–70; Dowdey, *Lee*, p. 144; Little Rock *Arkansas State Gazette*, 24 Aug. 1861.

CHAPTER SIX

1. The organizations of the two armies are printed in *OR*, vol. 10, pt. 2, pp. 548–51; vol. 11, pt. 2, pp. 483–89; vol. 20, pt. 2, pp. 413–15, 418–20, 425, 431–32; vol. 21, pp. 538–45; vol. 29, pt. 2, pp. 682–91; vol. 30, pt. 2, pp. 11–20; vol. 36, pt. 1, pp. 1021–27, and pt. 2, pp. 207–10; vol. 38, pt. 3, pp. 638–46. Krick's listing of units in the Army of Northern Virginia is in *Lee's Colonels*, pp. 439–62.

The data for the spring of 1862 include the troops from the Department of North Carolina who were then serving with the Army of Northern Virginia and the troops of the Army of the West who were then with the Army of Tennessee. The data for the Army of Tennessee for the fall of 1862 include the troops of Major General E. Kirby Smith, but they do not include the cavalry brigade of Brigadier General Nathan B. Forrest for which no organization was reported. The 1863 data for the Army of Northern Virginia do not include any troops from the Department of North Carolina, but they do include men in the Department of Richmond. The 1863 data for the Army of Tennessee exclude Lieutenant General James Longstreet's troops, who were temporarily sent for duty in the West.

The data for both 1863 and 1864 count consolidated units as one unit. For example, the Sixth and Ninth Tennessee regiments are counted as two units for the early period of the war but as only one unit after they were consolidated. Counting consolidated units as two or three units increases slightly the percentage of western units in the Army of Tennessee; it has no meaningful effect on the distribution of units in the Army of Northern Virginia.

The 1864 data include the forces in the Richmond-Petersburg lines as part of the Army of Northern Virginia and the units from the Department of Alabama, Mississippi, and East Louisiana that were transferred to Georgia for the Atlanta Campaign as part of the Army of Tennessee.

Companies from a regiment in either army that were operating with the army but independently of their regiment are not counted as separate units.

As with all statistical data, one could manipulate the raw figures and produce slightly different percentages. (By counting as one unit the four companies of the Washington Artillery of New Orleans, for example, one could decrease the number and percentage of western units in the Army of Northern Virginia.) Such differences, however, would not be great enough to alter the fundamental fact that the data in the text make clear: the Army of Northern Virginia was eastern; the Army of Tennessee was western.

2. The classic account of a Confederate soldier's experience going off to war (as well as all other aspects of a Rebel's life in the army) is Wiley, *Life of Johnny Reb*, pp. 15–27; Catton, *Hallowed Ground*, pp. 23, 44, 74. See also Nevins, *Improvised War*, pp. 159–61.

3. Freeman, *Lee's Lieutenants*, 1:709; *Nashville Patriot*, 13 Feb. 1861. Only New York's 164 officers exceeded Virginia's total of 137; Pennsylvania was in third place with 130. Not all of the Southern officers went with the Confederacy, of course, nor did all of the Northern officers remain loyal to the Union. Unfortunately, we have only the total figures. We do not know which officers were credited to each state in the 1861 count.

4. Basic biographical information on all Confederate generals is in Warner, *Generals in Gray*. There were, however, several men who had been born in the eastern Confederate states and by 1861 were associated with the West and became field grade officers in the Army of Tennessee. Samuel W. Ferguson, born in South Carolina, who served with the Twenty-eighth Mississippi Cavalry, is one example. At least five eastern officers resigned from the United States Army in 1861 and held positions as staff officers with the western army (Thomas Jordan, William W. Kirkland, Lunsford L. Lomax, Dabney H. Maury, and James E. Slaughter). I wish to thank Dick Sommers, who did yeoman work in identifying these men.

5. Watkins, *"Co. Aytch,"* pp. 184–85; Freeman, *Lee's Lieutenants*, 1:701; Wallace, *Guide to Virginia Military Organizations*, pp. 234–81; U.S. Congress, House of Representatives, "Militia of the United States."

6. Krick, *Lee's Colonels*, p. 18; Krick to author, 29 Apr. 1987, giving additions to the totals in the second edition of his work; *OR*, vol. 38, pt. 5, p. 793.

7. These data include only men who attended VMI up through the Class of 1862, which was graduated in 1861 so as to send the cadets off to the army.

8. Couper, *One Hundred Years at V.M.I.*, 3:11, 4:115. Couper's figures are traditionally accepted by authorities at VMI. I believe that they are inaccurate, but at present I do not have better ones. I am currently working on a study of VMI and its alumni in the Civil War. See my paper *"In Bello Praesidium."*

9. *Lynchburg Daily Virginian*, 30 Apr. 1861; Wallace, *Guide to Virginia*

Military Organizations, pp. 229–31; Riggs, " 'Put the Boys In,' " pp. 24–25, 28–32.

10. Freeman, quoted in Couper, *One Hundred Years at V.M.I.*, 2:106; Wallace, *Guide to Virginia Military Organizations*, p. 229.

11. Jim Moody of Charleston, South Carolina (in a telephone conversation with author, 18 Sept. 1987), who is studying the Citadel's role in the Civil War, agrees that more Citadel men served with the Army of Northern Virginia than with the Army of Tennessee, although he does not at present have exact figures. That many South Carolina units spent much of the war serving along the South Atlantic Coast meant that the relative proportion of Citadel men serving in the Army of Northern Virginia was less than the proportion of VMI alumni in the eastern army. In the 1830s, 1840s, and 1850s, furthermore, there had been a great emigration of South Carolinians to the states of the Old Southwest. For that reason, Moody believes, the relative proportion of Citadel alumni in the Army of Tennessee was much greater than the relative proportion of VMI men who served in that army. (As a VMI alumnus, I am tempted to list the presence of relatively more Citadel men in the Army of Tennessee as yet another millstone around the neck of the Rebels' unfortunate western army.)

12. Quoted in Couper, *One Hundred Years at V.M.I.*, 2:105.

CHAPTER SEVEN

1. I have classified the generals by the state from which they were appointed or by the state with which they were most closely associated in 1861 and not by their state of birth. Thus, for example, Braxton Bragg, who had been born in North Carolina but who had lived for several years in Louisiana before the war, is counted as a Louisiana—and hence western—general. For a listing of the generals and the states to which I have credited them, see the Appendix.

2. Thomas J. "Stonewall" Jackson had been graduated from West Point in 1846 and compiled a distinguished record in the Mexican War before resigning from the army to teach at the Virginia Military Institute, where, among other duties, he instructed the cadets in artillery tactics.

3. The organizations of the two armies on the dates indicated are in the *OR* on the pages cited in Chapter 6, note 1. For some reason, only twenty-two of the generals of the Army of Tennessee were listed on that army's return for late 1862. That small sample makes a statement of comparison on that date meaningless. As always, one could get other numbers by selecting other dates or by counting, for example, brigade commanders rather than

brigadier generals. Such changes, however, would not alter the conclusions drawn in the text.

4. Information on the generals is taken from Boatner's *Civil War Dictionary* and from Warner's *Generals in Gray* and, occasionally, from biographies and other sources. See the Appendix.

5. *OR*, vol. 51, pt. 2, p. 22; Freeman, *Lee*, 1:486–87; Connelly, *Army of the Heartland*, p. 37.

6. Connelly, *Army of the Heartland*, pp. 30–31, 46–47, 115, 124, 146, 178, 193, 205, 223; Connelly, *Autumn of Glory*, pp. 21, 30, 53, 81, 89, 106, 123–28, 155, 171–72.

7. Freeman, *Lee's Lieutenants*, 1:xv, 3:xxii–xxv.

8. On Freeman see Gignilliat, "Douglas Southall Freeman," and "A Historian's Dilemma"; and Williams, "Freeman." On Connelly, see the Preface to his *Army of the Heartland*, pp. vii–viii, and his Foreword, in McDonough and Connelly, *Five Tragic Hours*, p. xi.

CHAPTER EIGHT

1. Henderson, *Stonewall Jackson*, pp. 598, 602; Connelly, *Autumn of Glory*, p. 430.

2. Connelly, *Army of the Heartland*, pp. 62, 129, 141, 146–48, 151. For a much more favorable view of Johnston, especially of his personal characteristics, see Roland, *Albert Sidney Johnston*. Roland points out that Johnston was liked, respected, and admired by most of those with whom he came in contact, that he had a fine military record, that he received many honors, and that there was even talk of nominating him for president in 1860. Roland also finds much to praise in Johnston's short stint as the western commander when he successfully bluffed the Federals into believing that his force was much larger than it was. Roland faults Johnston, however, for his failure to save the thousands of troops he lost along the Tennessee and Cumberland rivers in early 1862. "He failed to act with the audacity and decision required by the crisis he faced," writes Roland, and he may have been "stunned and paralyzed" by those defeats. Johnston, Roland believes, recovered from these blows, pulled his forces together, and performed very well in the weeks immediately preceding his death.

3. Connelly, *Army of the Heartland*, pp. 129–30, 140, 176, 183; Connelly, *Autumn of Glory*, pp. 5, 431–32; Williams, *Beauregard*, pp. 34, 94, 101–8, 474.

4. Connelly, *Army of the Heartland*, pp. 205–6, 228, 231–32; Connelly, *Autumn of Glory*, pp. 70–72; Williams, *Beauregard*, p. 47; McWhiney, *Braxton Bragg and Confederate Defeat*.

5. Connelly, *Autumn of Glory*, pp. 102–3, 286, 288, 365, 369–71, 405, 519, 520; McMurry, "*'Enemy* at Richmond'"; Freeman, *Lee's Lieutenants*, 1:136n. Govan and Livingood, *A Different Valor*, is much more favorable to Johnston.

6. Connelly, *Autumn of Glory*, pp. 6, 322, 417, 429, 432; McMurry, *John Bell Hood and the War for Southern Independence*. Connelly's evaluations of the Rebel commanders in the West raise the question of the quality of Federal leadership in the region. If the western Rebel leaders were so bad, why did it take the Yankees four years to defeat them? Have Grant, Sherman, and Thomas been overrated? Fortunately, such questions are beyond the scope of this essay.

7. See Thomas, *American War and Peace*, p. 141; Freeman, *Lee's Lieutenants*, 1:606–14, 2:258–59, 510–14, and passim.

8. Connelly, *Army of the Heartland*, pp. 223, 248; Connelly, *Autumn of Glory*, pp. 21–22, 76, 91, 133, 146, 154, 234–78, 314–15, 365; *OR*, vol. 31, pt. 3, p. 209; McMurry, *John Bell Hood and the War for Southern Independence*, pp. 136–37, 152–53, 187–88.

9. McMurry, "*'Enemy* at Richmond,'" p. 16, and passim; Williams, *Beauregard*, pp. 201–2.

10. Lee's wartime letters are in Dowdey and Manarin, eds., *Wartime Papers of R. E. Lee*; see pp. 487–89 for the letter quoted in the text. See also the comments in Davis, *Deep Waters of the Proud*, pp. 174–75.

11. *OR*, vol. 32, pt. 2, pp. 537–38, 563–64; McMurry, "*'Enemy* at Richmond,'" p. 24.

12. *OR*, vol. 38, pt. 4, pp. 736, 745; Dowdey and Manarin, eds., *Wartime Papers of R. E. Lee*, pp. 745–55. Albert Sidney Johnston was a close personal friend of Davis and made a greater effort to alert the Richmond authorities to the situation in the West than did his successors.

13. The unnamed Virginian is quoted by Albert Castel in his forthcoming work that is presently titled "1864: Atlanta, Savannah, Nashville," p. 42. A draft of this work was available to the author. For a short but very important evaluation of Lee's role as a strategist, see Roland, "Generalship of Robert E. Lee," pp. 46–48.

CHAPTER NINE

1. Many of the issues debated by Connelly and Castel had been discussed in one form or another by earlier writers, especially by T. Harry Williams in *Beauregard* and "Freeman."

2. Connelly, "Robert E. Lee and the Western Confederacy."

3. Castel, "The Historian and the General." Castel, in turn, was assailed

by Richard F. Lemal in a "Communication," which also includes Castel's brief comment on Lemal's criticism of his criticism of Connelly's criticism of Lee.

4. Connelly and Jones, *Politics of Command*, pp. 31–48.

5. Connelly, "The Image and the General."

6. Connelly, *Marble Man*. Anyone who has read even cursorily in the letters and diaries of nineteenth-century Southerners—or, indeed, of nineteenth-century Christians—will realize that belief in one's own sinful nature and unworthiness was not unique to Lee. Connelly, of course, is aware of this fact, but he believes that Lee carried such attitudes to an extreme. For another perspective on Lee's boldness see John Morgan Dederer, "The Origins of Robert E. Lee's Bold Generalship." Dederer believes that Lee's boldness stemmed from his experiences in the Mexican War; from a study of Napoleon's campaigns; and from the example of his father, General Henry ("Light Horse Harry") Lee, who fought in the War for Independence.

7. Connelly and Bellows, *God and General Longstreet*, pp. 73–106.

8. Connelly, *Army of the Heartland*, p. 529.

9. Dowdey and Manarin, eds., *Wartime Papers of R. E. Lee*, p. 293. Connelly, "Robert E. Lee and the Western Confederacy," p. 122, ignores the qualifications that Lee used and calls this a suggestion "that the Army of Tennessee be sent to hold Richmond while he invaded Maryland."

10. Connelly and Jones, *Politics of Command*, pp. 72–82. For some provocative comments on a western concentration by the Rebels, see Roland, "Generalship of Robert E. Lee," pp. 46–48.

11. This statement is based on the assumption that the Confederates had to act to win their independence. Merely to fight a delaying action in the hope that the Northerners would grow tired of the war and allow the South to leave the Union was unrealistic. It assumes that the Southern generals in the West were skillful enough to avoid losing the war while they waited for the Yankees to run out of patience, that the Southern people would have remained steadfast in their support of the Confederacy, that Lincoln would have been willing to give up his goal of preserving the Union or that he could have been defeated in the 1864 election by a candidate who would have been willing to recognize the independence of the Confederacy, and that a nation that could not exercise patience at Fort Sumter in April 1861 or with regard to Kentucky's "neutrality" that fall would somehow have acquired the discipline and patience necessary to wage a protracted war that would have been far more psychological and political than military.

Bibliography

Official and Semiofficial Records and Documents

Booth, Andrew B., comp. *Records of Louisiana Confederate Soldiers and Louisiana Confederate Commands.* 3 vols. New Orleans, 1920.

Clark, Walter, ed. *Histories of the Several Regiments and Battalions from North Carolina in the Great War, 1861–65.* 4 vols. Raleigh and Goldsboro, 1901.

Henderson, Lillian, comp. *Rosters of Confederate Soldiers of Georgia, 1861–1865.* 7 vols. Hapeville, Ga., n.d.

Jones, Charles C., Jr. Compiled Service Record. National Archives (microfilm copy in Georgia Department of Archives and History).

Manarin, Louis H., and Weymouth T. Jordan, Jr., eds. *North Carolina Troops, 1861–1865: A Roster.* 11 vols. to date. Raleigh, 1966– .

[Tennessee] Civil War Centennial Commission. *Tennesseans in the Civil War: A Military History of Confederate and Union Units with Available Rosters of Personnel.* 2 vols. Nashville, 1964.

U.S. Bureau of the Census. *Census of 1860.* 4 vols. Washington, 1864–66.

U.S. Civil War Centennial Commission. *The Civil War: A Report to the Congress.* Washington, 1968.

U.S. Congress, House of Representatives. Militia of the United States. In *House Executive Document 58.* 37th Cong., 2d sess.

U.S. War Department, comp. *The War of the Rebellion: A Compilation of the Official Records of the Union and Confederate Armies.* 128 vols. Washington, 1880–1902.

Books and Articles

Adams, Michael C. C. *Our Masters the Rebels: A Speculation on Union Military Failure in the East, 1861–1865.* Cambridge, Mass., 1978.

Alexander, E. Porter. *Military Memoirs of a Confederate.* New York, 1907.

Aliyetti, John E. "From Brandy Station to Gettysburg—A Perspective." *Virginia Country's Civil War Quarterly* 8 (March 1987): 7–8.

Ambler, Charles H. *A History of West Virginia.* New York, 1933.

Ambrose, Stephen. *Halleck, Lincoln's Chief of Staff.* Baton Rouge, 1962.

Anderson, Hans Christian. *Rebellion in Missouri, 1861: Nathaniel Lyon and His Army of the West.* Philadelphia, 1961.

Bibliography

Baker, Jean H. *The Politics of Continuity: Maryland Political Parties from 1850 to 1870.* Baltimore, 1973.

Bean, W. G. *Stonewall's Man: Sandie Pendleton.* Chapel Hill, 1959.

Beringer, Richard E., Herman Hattaway, Archer Jones, and William N. Still, Jr. *Why the South Lost the Civil War.* Athens, Ga., 1986.

Black, Robert C. *Railroads of the Confederacy.* Chapel Hill, 1952.

Boatner, Mark Mayo III. *The Civil War Dictionary.* New York, 1959.

Boney, F. Nash. *John Letcher of Virginia: The Story of Virginia's Civil War Governor.* University, Ala., 1966.

Brewer, James H. *The Confederate Negro: Virginia's Craftsmen and Military Laborers, 1861–1865.* Durham, N.C., 1969.

Brown, Kent Masterson. "Lee at Gettysburg: The Man, the Myth, the Recriminations." *Virginia Country's Civil War Quarterly* 5 (1986): 13–26.

Cappon, Lester J. "Trend of the Southern Iron Industry under the Plantation System." *Journal of Economic and Business History* 2 (1929–30): 379–81.

Castel, Albert. "1864: Atlanta, Savannah, Nashville." Manuscript, 1987.

———. "The Historian and the General: Thomas L. Connelly versus Robert E. Lee." *Civil War History* 16 (1970): 50–63.

Catton, Bruce. *This Hallowed Ground: The Story of the Union Side of the Civil War.* New York, 1955.

Clark, Charles B. "Suppression and Control of Maryland, 1861–1865." *Maryland Historical Magazine* 54 (1959): 241–71.

Coddington, Edwin B. *The Gettysburg Campaign: A Study in Command.* New York, 1968.

Connelly, Thomas Lawrence. *Army of the Heartland: The Army of Tennessee, 1861–1862.* Baton Rouge, 1967.

———. *Autumn of Glory: The Army of Tennessee, 1862–1865.* Baton Rouge, 1971.

———. *Civil War Tennessee: Battles and Leaders.* Knoxville, 1979.

———. "The Image and the General: Robert E. Lee in American Historiography." *Civil War History* 19 (1973): 50–64.

———. *The Marble Man: Robert E. Lee and His Image in American Society.* New York, 1977.

———. "Robert E. Lee and the Western Confederacy: A Criticism of Lee's Strategic Ability." *Civil War History* 15 (1969): 116–32.

Connelly, Thomas Lawrence, and Barbara L. Bellows. *God and General Longstreet: The Lost Cause and the Southern Mind.* Baton Rouge, 1982.

Connelly, Thomas Lawrence, and Archer Jones. *The Politics of Command: Factions and Ideas in Confederate Strategy.* Baton Rouge, 1973.

Cooke, John Esten. *A Life of Gen. Robert E. Lee.* New York, 1871.

———. *The Life of Stonewall Jackson.* New York, 1863.

———. *Mohun, A Novel*. New York, 1868.

———. *Surry of Eagle's Nest; or the Memoirs of a Staff Officer Serving in Virginia*. New York, 1866.

———. *Wearing of the Gray: Being Personal Portraits, Scenes and Adventures of the War*. New York, 1865.

Cooling, Benjamin Franklin. *Forts Henry and Donelson: The Key to the Confederate Heartland*. Knoxville, 1987.

Cornish, Dudley T. *The Sable Arm: Negro Troops in the Union Army, 1861–1865*. New York, 1966.

Coulter, E. Merton. *The Civil War and Readjustment in Kentucky*. Chapel Hill, 1926.

———. *The Confederate States of America, 1861–1865*. Baton Rouge, 1950.

Couper, William. *One Hundred Years at V.M.I.* 4 vols. Richmond, 1939.

Curry, Richard O. *A House Divided: A Study of Statehood Politics and the Copperhead Movement in West Virginia*. Pittsburgh, 1964.

Daniel, Larry J. *Cannoneers in Gray: The Field Artillery of the Army of Tennessee, 1861–1865*. Tuscaloosa, Ala., 1984.

Davis, Archie K. *Boy Colonel of the Confederacy: The Life and Times of Henry King Burgwyn, Jr.* Chapel Hill, 1985.

Davis, William C. *Battle at Bull Run: A History of the First Major Campaign of the Civil War*. New York, 1977.

———. *The Battle of New Market*. Baton Rouge, 1975.

———. *The Deep Waters of the Proud*. Vol. 1 of *The Imperiled Union, 1861–1865*. 2 vols. to date. New York, 1982, 1983.

Dederer, John Morgan. "The Origins of Robert E. Lee's Bold Generalship: A Reinterpretation." *Military Affairs* 46 (1985): 117–23.

Douglas, Henry Kyd. *I Rode with Stonewall*. Chapel Hill, 1940.

Dowdey, Clifford. *Lee*. Boston, 1965.

Dowdey, Clifford, and Louis H. Manarin, eds. *The Wartime Papers of R. E. Lee*. Boston, 1961.

Eggleston, George Cary. *A Rebel's Recollections*. New York, 1875.

Fair, Charles. *From the Jaws of Victory*. New York, 1971.

Fishwick, Marshall W. *Virginia: A New Look at the Old Dominion*. New York, 1959.

Fiske, John. *The Mississippi Valley in the Civil War*. Boston, 1900.

Floan, Howard R. *The South in Northern Eyes, 1831–1861*. New York, 1958.

Freeman, Douglas Southall. *Lee's Lieutenants: A Study in Command*. 3 vols. New York, 1942–44.

———. *R. E. Lee: A Biography*. 4 vols. New York, 1934–35.

Frye, Dennis E. *2d Virginia Infantry*. Lynchburg, 1984.

Gallagher, Gary. "In the Shadow of Stonewall Jackson: Richard S. Ewell in the Gettysburg Campaign." *Virginia Country's Civil War Quarterly* 5 (1986): 54–59.

Georg, Kathleen R. "Where Was Pickett during Pickett's Charge? *Virginia Country's Civil War Quarterly* 11 (1987): 25–33.

Gignilliat, John L. "Douglas Southall Freeman." In Clyde N. Wilson, ed., *Dictionary of Literary Biography,* 17:157–69. Detroit, 1983.

————. "A Historian's Dilemma: A Posthumous Footnote for Freeman's *R. E. Lee.*" *Journal of Southern History* 43 (1977): 217–36.

Glatthaar, Joseph T. *The March to the Sea and Beyond: Sherman's Troops in the Savannah and Carolinas Campaign.* New York, 1985.

Goff, Richard D. *Confederate Supply.* Durham, N.C., 1969.

Govan, Gilbert E., and James W. Livingood. *A Different Valor: The Story of General Joseph E. Johnston, C.S.A.* Indianapolis, 1956.

Grant, Ulysses S. *Personal Memoirs.* 2 vols. New York, 1885.

Green, Russell P. "A. P. Hill's Manic Depression." *Virginia Country's Civil War Quarterly* 4, no. 1 (1986): 65–69.

Gruver, Rebecca Brooks. *An American History.* 2 vols. 2d ed. Reading, Mass., 1976.

Harrison, Lowell. *The Civil War in Kentucky.* Lexington, 1975.

Harwell, Richard B., and Philip N. Racine, eds. *The Fiery Trail: A Union Officer's Account of Sherman's Last Campaign.* Knoxville, 1986.

Hassler, Warren W., Jr. *Commanders of the Army of the Potomac.* Baton Rouge, 1962.

Hassler, William Woods. *A. P. Hill: Lee's Forgotten General.* Richmond, 1957.

————. "A. P. Hill at Gettysburg: How Did He Measure Up as Stonewall Jackson's Successor?" *Virginia Country's Civil War Quarterly* 5 (1986): 48–53.

————. *Colonel John Pelham: Lee's Boy Artillerist.* Richmond, 1960.

Hattaway, Herman, and Archer Jones. *How the North Won: A Military History of the Civil War.* Urbana, 1983.

Henderson, G. F. R. *Stonewall Jackson and the American Civil War.* 1898. Reprint. New York, 1955.

Hewitt, Lawrence L. *Port Hudson: Confederate Bastion on the Mississippi.* Baton Rouge, 1987.

Horn, Stanley F. *The Army of Tennessee: A Military History.* Indianapolis, 1941.

————, ed. and comp. *Tennessee's War: 1861–1865, Described by Participants.* Knoxville, 1965.

Johnston, Angus III. *Virginia Railroads in the Civil War.* Chapel Hill, 1961.

Johnston, Joseph E. *Narrative of Military Operations Directed during the Late War between the States.* Bloomington, 1959.

Bibliography

Jones, Charles C., Jr. *Historical Sketch of the Chatham Artillery during the Confederate War for Independence.* Albany, N.Y., 1867.

Jones, Robert H. *Disrupted Decades: The Civil War and Reconstruction Years.* New York, 1973.

Jones, Virgil Carrington. *Eight Hours before Richmond.* New York, 1957.

_____. *Ranger Mosby.* Chapel Hill, 1944.

Krick, Robert K. "'I Consider Him a Humbug . . .'—McLaws on Longstreet at Gettysburg." *Virginia Country's Civil War Quarterly* 5 (1986): 28–30.

_____. *Lee's Colonels: A Biographical Register of the Field Officers of the Army of Northern Virginia.* 2d ed. Dayton, 1984.

Krolick, Marshall D. "George Gordon Meade." *Blue & Gray* 5 (November 1987): 11–12.

Lemal, Richard F. "Communication." *Civil War History* 17 (1971): 171–74.

_____. "Lee and Longstreet at Gettysburg." *Virginia Country's Civil War Quarterly* 5 (1986): 32–40.

McDonough, James Lee. *Chattanooga: Death Grip on the Confederacy.* Knoxville, 1984.

_____. "Cold Days in Hell: The Battle of Stones River." *Civil War Times Illustrated* 25 (June 1986): 29–30.

_____. *Shiloh: In Hell before Night.* Knoxville, 1977.

_____. *Stones River: Bloody Winter in Tennessee.* Knoxville, 1980.

McDonough, James Lee, and Thomas Lawrence Connelly. *Five Tragic Hours: The Battle of Franklin.* Knoxville, 1983.

McDonough, James Lee, and James Pickett Jones. *War So Terrible: Sherman and Atlanta.* New York, 1987.

McElroy, John. *The Struggle for Missouri.* Washington, 1909.

McFeely, William S. *Grant: A Biography.* New York, 1981.

McMurry, Richard M. "'The *Enemy* at Richmond': Joseph E. Johnston and the Confederate Government." *Civil War History* 27 (1981): 5–31.

_____. "'*In Bello Praesidium*': The Virginia Military Institute in the Civil War." Unpublished paper. Copy in the Preston Library, Virginia Military Institute, Lexington.

_____. *John Bell Hood and the War for Southern Independence.* Lexington, Ky., 1982.

_____. "The Opening Phase of the 1864 Campaign in the West." *Atlanta Historical Journal* 27 (Summer 1983): 5–24.

McPherson, James M. *Ordeal by Fire: The Civil War and Reconstruction.* New York, 1982.

McWhiney, Grady. *Braxton Bragg and Confederate Defeat.* New York, 1969.

McWhiney, Grady, and Perry D. Jamieson. *Attack and Die: Civil War Military Tactics and the Southern Heritage.* University, Ala., 1982.

Bibliography

Manakee, Harold R. *Maryland in the Civil War.* Baltimore, 1959.

Milham, Charles G. *Gallant Pelham: American Extraordinary.* Washington, 1959.

Milligan, John D. *Gunboats down the Mississippi.* Annapolis, 1965.

Myers, Robert Manson, ed. *The Children of Pride: A True Story of Georgia and the Civil War.* New Haven, 1972.

Nevins, Allan. *The Improvised War, 1861–1862.* Vol. 1 of *The War for the Union.* New York, 1959.

North, Douglass C. *The Economic Growth of the United States, 1790–1860.* New York, 1966.

Norton, Mary Beth, et al. *A People and a Nation: A History of the United States.* Brief ed. 2 vols. Boston, 1984. 2d ed. 2 vols. Boston, 1986.

Norton, Oliver W. *The Attack and Defense of Little Round Top, Gettysburg, July 2, 1863.* New York, 1913.

O'Connor, Thomas H. *The Disunited States: The Era of Civil War and Reconstruction.* 2d ed. New York, 1978.

Parrish, William E. *A History of Missouri.* Vol. 3: *1860–1875.* Columbia, 1973.

———. *Turbulent Partnership: Missouri and the Union, 1861–1865.* Columbia, 1963.

Pfanz, Harry W. *Gettysburg: The Second Day.* Chapel Hill, 1987.

Randall, James G. *The Civil War and Reconstruction.* Boston, 1953.

Randall, James G., and David Donald. *The Civil War and Reconstruction.* 2d ed. Boston, 1966.

Reed, Rowena. *Combined Operations in the Civil War.* Annapolis, 1978.

Riggs, David F. " 'Put the Boys In.' " *Civil War Times Illustrated* 18 (January 1980): 24–32.

Robertson, James I., Jr. *A. P. Hill: The Story of a Confederate Warrior.* New York, 1987.

Roland, Charles P. *Albert Sidney Johnston: Soldier of Three Republics.* Austin, 1964.

———. "The Generalship of Robert E. Lee." In Grady McWhiney, ed. *Grant, Lee, Lincoln and the Radicals: Essays on Civil War Leadership,* pp. 31–71. New York, 1966.

Russell, William H. *My Diary North and South.* Edited by Fletcher Pratt. New York, 1954.

Sellers, Charles, et al. *A Synopsis of American History.* 6th ed. Boston, 1985.

Shanks, Henry T. *The Secession Movement in Virginia, 1847–1861.* Richmond, 1934.

Siepel, Kevin H. *Rebel: The Life and Times of John Singleton Mosby.* New York, 1983.

Smith, Gordon B. *The Chatham Artillery, 1786–1986.* Savannah, 1985.

Bibliography

Sommers, Richard J. *Richmond Redeemed: The Siege at Petersburg.* New York, 1981.

Sorrell, G. Moxley. *Recollections of a Confederate Staff Officer.* New York, 1905.

Stein, Jess, ed. *The Random House Dictionary.* New York, 1978.

Stewart, George R. *Pickett's Charge: A Microhistory of the Final Attack at Gettysburg, July 3, 1863.* Boston, 1959.

Swinton, William. *Campaigns of the Army of the Potomac.* New York, 1882.

Taylor, William R. *Cavalier and Yankee: The Old South and American National Character.* New York, 1961.

Temple, Oliver P. *East Tennessee and the Civil War.* New York, 1971.

Thomas, Emory M. *The American War and Peace, 1860–1877.* Englewood Cliffs, N.J., 1973.

Tindall, George Brown. *America: A Narrative History.* New York, 1984.

Townsend, William H. *Lincoln and the Bluegrass: Slavery and Civil War in Kentucky.* Lexington, Ky., 1955.

Vandiver, Frank E. *Rebel Brass: The Confederate Command System.* Baton Rouge, 1956.

_____. *Their Tattered Flags: The Epic of the Confederacy.* New York, 1970.

Walker, Peter Franklin. "Building a Tennessee Army: Autumn, 1861." *Tennessee Historical Quarterly* 16 (1957): 99–116.

Wallace, Lee A., Jr. *1st Virginia Infantry.* Lynchburg, 1984.

_____. *A Guide to Virginia Military Organizations, 1861–1865.* Lynchburg, 1986.

Ward, John William. *Andrew Jackson, Symbol for an Age.* New York, 1953.

Warner, Ezra J. *Generals in Blue: Lives of the Union Commanders.* Baton Rouge, 1964.

_____. *Generals in Gray: Lives of the Confederate Commanders.* Baton Rouge, 1959.

Watkins, Sam R. *"Co. Aytch," Maury Grays, First Tennessee Regiment, or, A Side Show of the Big Show.* Nashville, 1881.

Watson, Ritchie Devon, Jr. *The Cavalier in Virginia Fiction.* Baton Rouge, 1985.

Wert, Jeffry. "Confederate Strategy." *Civil War Times Illustrated* 26 (March 1987): 44–45.

Wiley, Bell I. *The Life of Johnny Reb: The Common Soldier of the Confederacy.* Indianapolis, 1943.

Williams, Kenneth P. *Lincoln Finds a General.* 5 vols. New York, 1949–56.

Williams, T. Harry. "Freeman, Historian of the Civil War: An Appraisal." *Journal of Southern History* 21 (1955): 91–100.

_____. *Lincoln and His Generals.* New York, 1952.

_____. *P. G. T. Beauregard: Napoleon in Gray.* Baton Rouge, 1955.

Bibliography

Wright, William C. *The Secession Movement in the Middle Atlantic States.* Rutherford, N.J., 1973.

Yearns, W. Buck, ed. *The Confederate Governors.* Athens, Ga., 1985.

Newspapers

Atlanta Southern Confederacy
Columbus Enquirer
Charleston Mercury
Little Rock Arkansas State Gazette
Lynchburg Virginian
Nashville Patriot
Richmond Dispatch
Richmond Whig
Savannah Morning News
Savannah Republican

Miscellaneous

Civil War Round Table Associates *Digest*, 15 (June 1984).

Hughes, Michael. Remarks on the Atlanta Campaign. Congress of Civil War Round Tables, Marietta, Georgia, 2 Oct. 1986.

Krick, Robert K. Letter to author, 29 April 1987.

Index

Adams, Daniel W. (CS general), 160

Adams, Henry (novelist), 50

Adams, John (CS general), 163

Adams, Michael C. C. (historian), 44–51

Adams, William W. (CS general), 161

Agrarian myth, 49

Alabama, 26, 70, 88, 158; war in, 16, 64

Alabama military units, 88, 90; 4th Inf., 102; 9th Inf., 95

Alabama, Mississippi, and East Louisiana, Confederate Department of, 65, 68, 70

Alexander, E. Porter (CS general), 8, 110, 159

Alexandria, Confederate Department of, 64

Allen, Henry W. (CS general), 160

Allen, William M. (CS general), 158

Ambrose, Stephen (historian), 52

"Anaconda plan," 53, 82

Anderson, George B. (CS general), 162

Anderson, George T. (CS general), 159

Anderson, James Patton (CS general), 159

Anderson, Joseph R. (CS general), 164

Anderson, Richard H. (CS general), 162

Anderson, Robert H. (CS general), 159

Anderson, Samuel R. (CS general), 163

Antietam (Md.), Battle of (1862), 153

Appalachian Mountains, 16–19

Appomattox, Confederate surrender at (1865), 2, 4

Archer, James J. (CS general), 161

Aristocracy, role in war of, 44–45, 46–47

Arkansas, 26, 84, 88, 98, 158

Arkansas military units: 3d Inf., 90; militia, 98

Armistead, Lewis A. (CS general), 94, 164

Armstrong, Frank G. (CS general), 158

"Army of Tennessee versus the Army of Northern Virginia, The," 140

Army of the Heartland: The Army of Tennessee, 1861–1862, 5

Ashby, Turner (CS general), 164

Atlanta, Ga., 28, 130

Atlanta Campaign (1864), ix, 64, 95–96, 129, 130, 136

Attack and Die: Civil War Military Tactics and the Southern Heritage, xiii

Baker, Alpheus (CS general), 158

Baker, Laurence S. (CS general), 162

Baldwin, William E. (CS general), 161

Ball's Bluff (Va.), Battle of (1861), 48

CPSIA information can be obtained
at www.ICGtesting.com
Printed in the USA
LVHW011109200721
693179LV00004B/352